Ice Cream for Breakfast

Ice Cream for Breakfast

If you follow all the rules, you miss half the fun

Leslie Levine

CB

CONTEMPORARY BOOKS

Library of Congress Cataloging-in-Publication Data

Levine, Leslie.
    Ice cream for breakfast : if you follow all the rules, you miss
half the fun / Leslie Levine.
       p.   cm.
    ISBN 0-8092-9865-1
    1. Conduct of life.   I. Title.
    BJ1581.2.L478   2001
    158—dc21   00-59015

Lyrics from Bruce Henderson's "Big Moon" printed by kind permission. Lyrics
copyright 1997 Senator Dog Music (ASCAP). From the CD by Bruce Henderson,
"The Wheels Roll" (Valley Entertainment).

Cover design by Kim Bartko
Cover illustration by Susy Pilgrim Waters
Interior design by Kim Bartko
Interior illustrations by Susy Pilgrim Waters

Published by Contemporary Books
A division of the McGraw-Hill Companies.
4255 West Touhy Avenue, Lincolnwood (Chicago), Illinois 60712-1975 U.S.A.
Copyright © 2001 by Leslie Levine
Printed in the United States of America
International Standard Book Number: 0-8092-9865-1
00 01 02 03 04 05 QM 15 14 13 12 11 10 9 8 7 6 5 4 3 2 1

To the memory of my grandmother

Minnie Bane (1907–2000)

And for Jon, Esther, and Philip.

With love.

contents

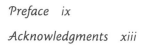

kiss
a
frog

Preface

"GIVE HER ICE CREAM FOR BREAKFAST—she'll never forget it." Nearly three years ago, a friend offered that sage advice as I prepared to take my daughter to Chicago. In a few months, we'd be moving from Upstate New York to the Midwest. I thought a weekend in our new hometown-to-be would help soften the blow of relocating.

As it turned out, ice cream for breakfast, room service, and an evening swim all contributed to the trip's success. In fact, I am convinced that it is our ability to bend the rules—to shift life's collective paradigms—that enables us to weather many of the challenges we confront on a daily basis. Bending the rules—or, in some cases, forgoing them completely—gives us a fresh perspective, shakes things up a bit, and forces us to see life through a slightly different lens. Altering the rules leads to ideas that ultimately can reshape the way we see ourselves. Breaking the rules also can be the perfect antidote to the powerful force of stress.

As I thought about the message I wanted to convey in *Ice Cream for Breakfast,* it occurred to me that a lot of the rules we follow—well, the ones we're supposed to follow anyway—are old. We learned them a long time ago, and in many cases, what served us well as kids doesn't necessarily mean it's good for us now. Of course some rules we couldn't live without—like looking both ways before we cross the street and wearing seat belts, which is such a good rule that it has become the law in a lot of places. But what about not getting dessert unless you've finished all your dinner?

That's torture. Or always having to go to bed at a certain time? On some nights, there's just too much to see and do.

As I began to write the book, I also realized that we sometimes leave too much behind as we progress into adulthood. Our thirst for adventure begins to wane. Rather than exciting us, the thrill of the unknown makes us anxious. We forget to nurture our imagination. We may stifle our tenacity and perseverance to the point that we actually take no for an answer. Even our capacity for uncontrollable laughter is somehow diminished by the rules that govern adulthood. Instead of giving ourselves permission to be joyful and do the things that make us happy, we arbitrarily create rules that prevent us from enjoying as much as we can. So instead of lingering in the tub (page 23), we bathe as fast as we can. Instead of celebrating our own birthdays (page 79), we minimize the day and let it pass almost unnoticed. These made-up rules may give us some order in the short-term but ultimately shortchange what could be a more fulfilling and fun life. Sometimes the easiest way to break these rules is to look at life through a child's eyes. Instead of dodging a sprinkler as it begins to wave in your direction, run through it, get a little wet, especially if it's a hot day. If you're hesitant, ask yourself what's the worst that can happen. Maybe an extra dry-cleaning bill, but wouldn't it be worth it?

Ice Cream for Breakfast is intended for anyone who's ever felt closed in by the rules. It's also meant to help you stay centered amid the frenzy that plagues our fast-paced lives. In "Do One Thing at a Time," for instance, you'll learn how to slow down a little. In some cases, you'll read about a rule that's particularly steeped in tradition, as in "Talk to Strangers." In other chapters, rules resurface and are given a new twist, like "Keep Your Eyes on Your Own

Paper," which addresses the importance of listening to your own voice. In all fifty-two chapters, one for each week of the year, I've tried to incorporate the universal experiences of childhood and render the memories into strategies that can enrich our lives as adults.

Ice Cream for Breakfast will introduce you to new ways to counter the pesky tyrannies that can sabotage your quest for happiness and fulfillment. As I worked on the book, I recalled some of my own unfettered joys of childhood. I include a few here along with the recollections typical, I think, of many adults. My hope is that the book will help you bring those good memories to life.

The core of *Ice Cream for Breakfast* is really found in a short phrase that I read in a recent E-mail. In my efforts to confirm the number of shooting stars that fall over the earth in one evening ("Make a Wish," page 154), I found a source whose wisdom goes far beyond his knowledge of the solar system. In a flurry of E-mails about shooting stars and making wishes, Piet Hut, a professor of astrophysics at Princeton University, referenced a Tibetan notion that states, "No hope, no fear." "No hope" refers to the limiting nature of specifying what you want versus keeping an open mind to all of life's possibilities. "No fear" suggests that you strip yourself of expectations, and, instead, be receptive to whatever comes your way. In four simple words, "No hope, no fear" seems to capture the spirit of *Ice Cream for Breakfast.* As you read these pages, remember that *Ice Cream for Breakfast* is not about "healing the child within" or "healing the inner child." Its message is simpler: be a kid again; fire up your imagination; become insatiably curious; use the skills you learned ages ago to help you enjoy the smaller moments in life—the priceless moments, the moments that we look forward to and then savor over and over again.

you
THANK
YOU
Thank you
Thank you
Thank you
Thank you
Thank you
Thank you
THANK YOU
THANK you
Thank you
Thank you
Thank you

Acknowledgments

THIS BOOK COULD NOT have been written without my talented editor and cherished friend Danielle Egan-Miller, whose support has been immeasurable; my good friend Christina Rossomando, who sustained me and listened intently for nearly a year; and my husband and best friend, Jon Levine, who continues to believe in me and provide support. Profound gratitude to Kim Bartko for her beautiful art direction; Marisa L'Heureux for her attention to detail and her dedication; and Denise Betts, Cori Spragg, Susan Jensen, and the entire team at Contemporary Books for their commitment and hard work. Special thanks, too, to the talented Susy Pilgrim Waters for her inspiring illustrations and to Eloise L. Kinney Schmich for reading the manuscript with the finest-tooth comb.

For their invaluable insights and steady encouragement many thanks to Sandy Beckwith, Robin LaBorwit, Victoria Moran, Phyllis Wagner, Pat DeLuca, Donna Greenberg, Judith Kalfon, Laura Levin, Pam Bernstein, Susan Ginsberg, Ann Marie Moriarty, Jerry Flach, Hope DeCederfelt, and Mitch Curren. Special thanks to Heidi Rosenberg for her generous support. Appreciation to Bill Thomas for paving the way to Bruce Henderson who, once again, has graciously shared his wonderful music. Many thanks to Deborah Durham for her unbounded generosity and her homemade ice cream. Warm thanks as well to Mary Ellen Blanchard for keeping my Mac alive and well and for her ongoing support.

For their continued support I would like to thank my mother, Elinor Zevin, my sister, Wendy Zevin, and my brother, Robert Zevin. Special thanks, too, to Helen and Jerry Levine, Sheri and Steve Levine, Cynthia Levin, and David Green.

Infinite love and gratitude to my children, Esther and Philip, who inspire and teach me every day.

1 Look at Your Beautiful Toes

"To say something nice about themselves, this is the hardest thing in the world for people to do. They'd rather take their clothes off."
—NANCY FRIDAY, *MY MOTHER/MY SELF* (1977)

ABOUT A MONTH AGO a friend marveled at my daughter's healthy self-esteem. My daughter, a nail-polish connoisseur (not unlike many of her peers), displayed her newly pedicured feet. "Look at my beautiful toes," she said.

"She didn't say, 'Aren't my toes beautiful?'" observed my friend. No, this girl knew her toes looked good and wanted to share her handiwork and enthusiasm. Of course *I* think her toes are beautiful—I have since the day she was born. Yet how many of us can comfortably point out our personal beauty marks without appearing conceited?

Her unabashed appreciation for simple beauty and her ability to speak the truth refreshingly broke one of the most restrictive rules I can think of and one that has dogged me since I was a small girl: don't call attention to yourself, and for goodness' sake, never, ever pay yourself a compliment.

Maybe that's why so many of us have trouble accepting praise from others. "Oh, this old thing? I've had it forever," you say as a friend admires a piece of jewelry or a sweater. "I feel so fat though," you may respond, as a well-meaning friend says you're looking great. How can two words—*thank-you*—be so hard to say? How on Earth could a simple response like *thank-you* cause such a stir?

Becoming comfortable with your physical assets—whether they're your beautiful toes; attractive ears; long, slender fingers; whatever—doesn't have to be so overwhelming. Think about it: in school we had to comprehend and sometimes memorize whole chapters of history, geography, math, and all sorts of complicated facts and figures. But "thank-you"? That's easy. Really. The nice thing about responding to a compliment with a "thank-you" or even "thanks" is its quick shelf life. It's the piece of conversation that can easily move you and someone else on to the next topic. It's short. It's sweet. It validates the other person's great taste, but more important—and more lasting—it becomes a personal gesture of self-approval. And remember, just because no one asks for your beauty secrets doesn't mean for a second that you're not beautiful.

Responding positively to a compliment is one of the easiest ways for us to be kind to ourselves. Of course, it is essential to be gracious and show appreciation for others. But it's equally important to recognize our own assets. It's true that outer beauty is, for the most part, a gift from Mother Nature, our parents' genes, and, in some cases, the result of artifice—an application of nail polish, the way a new haircut falls, or even the controversial, though commonplace, pull and tuck. Nonetheless, just as you'd say "thank-you" when someone admires your hard work or generosity, it's OK to respond similarly when the object of admiration is something connected to your inner or outer beauty.

Perhaps the prerequisite—the class you must first complete before graduating to "thank-you"—is developing the courage to ask those around you to "look at your beautiful toes." I want you to pass this course, so if at first it comes out as a question, as in "Aren't my toes beautiful?" that's OK. After all, many of us have a lot to unlearn. And don't worry about standards. Few of us can match the airbrushed images offered up by Fifth Avenue. Yet no one can corner the market on inner beauty, which is where our self-esteem is born. Water it well and give it plenty of sunshine. It's yours to discover and nurture. Even your feet will emit a shimmering glow.

Quick-Fix Beauty Treatments

One of the nicest—and easiest—ways to feel beautiful is to indulge yourself with a quick-fix beauty treatment. Opportunities abound, and the results are, well, beautiful. Visit your favorite cosmetic counter for a makeover. Don't feel pressured into buying anything; just show your appreciation for the new you and say, "I'll think about it." Of course, an occasional purchase offers a lovely high. Buy yourself a hat, one that nicely frames your beautiful face and protects you from the elements. Get yourself a manicure for no special reason other than you're worth it. Dig out an old piece of jewelry and wear it like new all over again. Create your own beauty potion with yummy fruit juices, yogurt, and a few ice cubes in a blender. Drink it and pat yourself on the back for eating something healthy. Just knowing you're doing something good for yourself will bring out your inner beauty. You'll see.

2 Do the Wrong Thing

"We are rather apt to consider an act wrong because it is unpleasant to us."
—GEORGE ELIOT, *MIDDLEMARCH* (1871)

IN SOME WAYS, *Ice Cream for Breakfast* is all about doing the wrong things—talking to strangers, eating foods that aren't good for you. Speaking simply, it is about breaking a rule here and there to give yourself a break. Doing the wrong thing implies a certain mischief, a risk, a chance to ignore convention and get away with it. As kids, most of us did the wrong things from time to time. Getting in trouble was just part of the game. We were told not to be late, but we came in after dark anyway. We were told to "just have one," but we grabbed a handful anyway. We were warned about the slippery floor, but we just had to slide. Sometimes we did the wrong things unintentionally, and escaping punishment was especially sweet. Other times, though, doing the wrong thing occurred with more spontaneity. We couldn't stop ourselves.

In some ways, things haven't changed. Although we rarely hear someone tell us to "do the wrong thing," we're still intrigued by, and a little attracted to, the chance to be disobedient. It's sort of an "I-dare-you-to" voice deep inside. It's the old conundrum that has the heart and the head in a heated battle. The heart tells you to take a chance on a new suitor. Your head, on the other hand, has seen it all before and wants more than anything to save you from the work required to mend a broken heart.

Whether it's a chance at romance or the urge to skip the nightly flossing routine, doing the wrong thing may be the right thing to do for yourself. The problem with doing the wrong thing, of course, is the subsequent guilt, an uncomfortable though inevitable outcome. But sometimes guilt is necessary; it can teach us how to behave in the world. If you hurt someone's feelings, for example, you may feel bad about it later. This is the good kind of guilt.

But there's also the bad guilt, the loaded-down weight of way too much responsibility, the little, yet powerful, voice that admonishes and says, "If you'd done such and such, this might not have ever happened." This is the sly and wicked guilt that can mercilessly chip away at your usual noble self. Like when you finally build up the nerve to say no when you're asked for the thousandth time to volunteer at the school. Or when you tell a friend that you don't have time for her right now but you will in a few days and you hope that will be OK. You may be on level ground when the words come out of your mouth, yet the image in your mind's eye might have you on a mountaintop, screaming out the words at the top of your lungs.

I'm not suggesting that you commit a criminal act or in any way disregard the laws that attempt to keep our society intact. I am proposing, however, allowing a little latitude when it comes to doing what's best for you. Singer-songwriter Bruce Henderson says this about his song "August": "There's a certain freedom in doing what you know is wrong. The pleasure is fleeting, sometimes lasting only as long as the moment of decision itself."

Indeed, the pleasure is derived from the momentary—longer in some cases—sense of letting go, of allowing ourselves be out of control. Don't drive through life hands free, but consider liberating yourself from the need to constantly hold the reins, to embrace only that over which you have total command. It's about letting go and acceptance.

Accepting your own definition of what's right and wrong is one of the hardest and most rewarding lessons you can teach yourself. What's clearly wrong for someone else may be what's positively correct for you. Accept the distinction and then stick with your convictions. You may learn to like it after all.

3 Just a Spoonful of Sugar

"Self-pity is the simplest luxury."

—Rita Mae Brown, *Bingo* (1988)

One afternoon, many years ago, I received a phone message from the nurse at my daughter's day camp. In the midst of a fishing expedition, a fishhook had somehow lodged itself into the heel of her foot. My own foot flinched when I heard those words. Antibiotic ointment had been applied, and she was resting "comfortably" in the office. Wondering how this could have happened and somewhat doubtful that anyone could be comfortable in this situation, I called the pediatrician's office. They'd be expecting us shortly.

Once the doctor had extracted the fishhook, I treated the patient to a manicure, because sometimes a painful experience (or the anticipation of one) calls for pampering and self-indulgence—that proverbial spoonful of sugar to help the medicine go down. Think of the toy drawer at the dentist's office or the milkshake after a root canal. Just the other day, as I scheduled my daughter's annual physical, she overheard me inquire about a shot, and she quickly looked up from her homework with one word: *manicure*. Ah, I thought; a new tradition takes hold.

The problem with physical pain is that many of us—regardless of the reward—were taught to endure and accept discomfort. But pain hurts, and just as you wouldn't lie to a child about a shot—"It won't hurt a bit"—it's wrong to deny your suffering.

Adding something sweet to an otherwise unpleasant experience is one way to accept the pain for what it is—annoying, excruciating, inconvenient, whatever—and then, later, to dilute the aftershock, the rippling that occurs with any wound. Thus, when-  ever we experience pain, we can look forward to a period of heal-ing—renewal, even. The spoonful of sugar is not unlike the bouquet of flowers sent to lift a friend's spirits or the pick-me-up purchase at your favorite boutique.

If you sweep your pain away, you commit a disservice to your-self and to others. Human pain—our frailty—is universal. The reason you can empathize and sympathize with someone's pain is because you have experienced it yourself. Rewarding yourself for enduring pain may seem like the ultimate self-pity celebration. But once in a while, feeling a little sorry for yourself really does help the medicine go down. Besides, you can't wait for others to chase your pain away. Sometimes you just have to take care of yourself.

As we get older, our aches and pains take up more time than we'd like. Sometimes, just a checkup is enough to make us feel like we're not well. Next time you go in for a mammogram or some other test, treat yourself to something special like a yummy coffee drink topped with whipped cream. Or buy yourself a nice pair of shoes. And for goodness' sake, follow up distressing dental appointments with your favorite flavor of milkshake or a new book. For every situation that's not particularly pleasant, give your-self a gift, something to make it all worthwhile, something that will remind you later that "it wasn't so bad after all."

Think of those annual dental exams. Wasn't the best part when you got to pick a prize? I remember with crystal-clear clarity a drawer filled to the brim with rings. Rubies, diamonds, real gold, I was sure. Whatever pain I had withstood and whatever accolades my mother and the dentist showered on me for my bravery, nothing made me feel better than reaching into that drawer for a fine piece of jewelry.

Even today, when my kids are offered a toy at the dentist's office, I am reminded of the extraordinary healing and soothing powers that can help settle the score with whatever ails us. You might even consider adopting the preventative strategy used by my friend Karen, who slips a spoonful of sugar into her daily latté. I think it's her way of starting the day on a sweet note—not a bad habit as far as I can see.

Sugar on the Wound

Here are some easy ways to ease the pain:

- Stock your medicine cabinet with Band-Aids usually reserved for kids; they're fun, colorful, and have a proven track record for hastening recovery.
- Send yourself a get-well card; you'll forget about it completely until it's delivered with the rest of your mail. You'll howl at your silliness.
- If you open your pantry and a can of food falls on your toe, call a friend and have a pity party.
- Recognize and accept the healing properties of chocolate.
- If your forehead feels warm, take two aspirin and a Popsicle.

4 Dear Diary

"I believe one writes because one has to create a world in which one can live."
—ANAÏS NIN, *THE DIARY OF ANAÏS NIN*, VOLUME 5 (1954)

Dear Diary:
Today was the worst day of my life. Everything that could go
wrong, did go wrong. I want to soak my head in the toilet.
Yours ever, Leslie

I REMEMBER WRITING LINES LIKE THAT. As a teenager, I wrote volumes. Tear stains and flattened four-leaf clovers are a testament to the refuge I sought in those pages. My diary was my friend.

A diary is where we stashed our true feelings, the feelings we couldn't—indeed, wouldn't—verbalize. For many of us, our diaries sat quietly under lock and key or lay mostly undisturbed (we hoped) inside a drawer. We'd know if it had been moved by even a quarter inch. We'd memorize its placement in the same way we learned by heart all those vocabulary words. If anyone had snooped around, we knew, and there'd be hell to pay.

Like other childhood joys we savored but gave up over time, writing in our diaries has turned into an extra—something we think about doing but can't necessarily justify because of other commitments, real and imagined. Writing down our feelings, our truest thoughts, seems like a luxury, almost selfish. Yet putting your innermost thoughts into words can be just as vital to a healthy lifestyle as good exercise and a nutritious diet.

Today, we call our diaries *journals*, repositories for our every emotion. A personal history we can review. A release so that our souls can breathe. Some journals are for specific times in our lives. The entries written about a baby's first year can later provide a nostalgic and touching reminder of the dramatic ways life changes in one twelve-month period. Others keep journals during the course of an illness; the writing provides a catharsis that can actually hasten recovery. Quite simply, journaling can get us through the best and worst of times.

Think of your entries as parts of an ongoing, private conversation. Allow every voice to speak—the doubter, the one who's afraid or angry, the optimist, the one who sees something good in each day. Journaling can help you understand your troubles. Indeed, keeping a diary may even help you write your way *out* of trouble.

Documenting our feelings is an important and accessible way to squeeze the stress out of our lives. It's also a means for self-exploration and growth.

Taking time to sit and open your journal—or even anticipating the moment when you'll have the time—is like tapping another source of oxygen or discovering an extra outlet for whatever's brewing inside. Writing it down also gives you the chance to try out your reactions. Let's face it: we don't always think before we act. In many cases, our dear diaries can keep us from behaving in ways that we might later regret. Like letters never sent, our journal entries reflect important and valid points of view. That they remain on a page and go no further does not lessen their power. Even if you decide to destroy what you write, the act of getting your thoughts out of your head is what really matters most.

Logging these unedited, first-draft-only passages can send you on an important, lifelong journey. In fact, your entries can lead you on two journeys. First, you record an event and the accompanying emotions. The second journey—when you review and reflect—is more like a pilgrimage during which you can travel within yourself. Sometimes, these journeys may contrast sharply with your original experience. It may feel as if someone has made a drastic change in your life script between the dress rehearsal and opening night. As jarring as this may feel, be glad for the difference, because very likely it will signal an inch or two of personal growth. This usually means you've taken the time to question your own beliefs.

As you record your life events and your reactions, you discover answers to some of the most important questions. The answers may sometimes surprise you and even disappoint. And, like me, you might even have those days when you want to soak your head in the toilet. When this happens, remember the refuge of your diary and let the writing pull you in and keep you a little more steady, a little more calm.

It won't always be easy to reach for your dear diary. As a writer, my instincts are to reread, cut, and edit. And reliving an unpleasant experience through the written word doesn't necessarily promise a perfect, nicely wrapped perspective. But life isn't perfect, and perspectives are rarely neatly packaged.

There is safety in the blank page. It is a clean slate, a chance to start again, a chance to understand. Don't worry about writing great prose or developing a literary masterpiece. Just try to see where you've been and where you might go next.

Become Enlightened by Your Written Words

Try this simple exercise to reap the benefits of keeping a journal: for a set period of time, a week or maybe even a month, promise yourself to write something on the odd days. Don't think of this as an assignment. Consider these days as opportunities to write down your observations, thoughts, and feelings. If you have a problem, for instance, and need to work it through, write down the situation, list your options, and express your emotions about each. If something truly wonderful occurs, use a special pen and write with lots of exclamation points and all caps. It will make your happy news that much bigger. If you're sad and can't share with a friend, fill a page with your thoughts and feel the weight of your sorrow lift ever so slightly. Write your thoughts in a decorative journal or in an old-fashioned spiral notebook. Don't forget to keep it someplace that's easy to reach, like your night table or dresser.

5 Laugh Like There's No Tomorrow

"A good time for laughing is when you can."
—JESSAMYN WEST, *EXCEPT FOR ME AND THEE* (1969)

I AM INDEBTED TO AND BLESSED BY the people who make me laugh. In their company I am like a cash register each time it's fed some coins and bills—"ka-ching, ka-ching": I'm a little richer, a little more fulfilled. Sometimes my laughter comes bubbling up from my toes. Or it emerges from somewhere soulful, a deep and holy place that is steeped in memory.

Some of the best laughter comes without warning. Not too long ago, I shared a few howls with my friend Donna as we heard our mundane, let's-get-up-to-date conversation nosedive into something positively X-rated. It was during one of our morning walks. She said one thing, I heard another, and eventually we crumbled into fits of uncontrollable and irreverent laughter. We were like two schoolgirls running around the playground, becoming more hysterical with every minute.

Sometimes laughter gets us into trouble. Have you ever attended a lecture or service when suddenly you were stricken with the most unbelievable urge to laugh out loud? Nothing—not even the most solemn moment you can imagine—can keep your laughter tethered down. When she was a kid, my friend Phyllis repeatedly tested one friend's restraint. In their Hebrew class, anyone could be asked to stand up to speak with absolutely no warning. Each time Anne's turn came around, she would hear the hushed murmurings of her friend. "Penis, bosom, penis, bosom . . ." Eventually, Anne could not contain her laughter, and time after time she was excused from the class. "I felt bad," says Phyllis, who still laughs at her antics. "But it was just so funny."

Some of the best laughs are the ones we steal, the ones that shock us and make us feel like we've gotten away with something really good. When my friend Danielle was about six or seven, she formed the "Swearing Club." Each afternoon as she and her foul-mouthed friend walked home, they'd call out every four-letter word they knew. These girls knew how to make themselves laugh. And like Phyllis, Danielle recounts her mischief with a silliness that seems to echo what the Swearing Club must have enjoyed so heartily.

When we hear ourselves laugh, we're able to gauge what's right in the world. In fact, listening for laughter is one way I try to quantify the joy around me. It's not unlike what I do to assess the soundness of my kids' diets. Rather than focus on one day, I look at how they've eaten over the course of a week. It's the same with laughter. If I don't hear it enough over the course of a few days, I'll know that our equilibrium is off and that we're just too stressed.

Sometimes we don't even realize the magnitude of our stress—we're so deeply immersed in it. But when we let a little laughter in, it's like shedding a strip of light into an otherwise darkened room—a glimpse of hope, a glimmer of possibility. Maybe you've attended a memorial service where, instead of witnessing a room of solemn mourners, you see people chattering and laughing. Conversation blends with food and drink, and, not surprisingly, you may forget for a moment why you're there in the first place. That, of course, is the point and the reason why we shouldn't be afraid to laugh even though we really feel like crying. It's a wonderful and, in many cases, a necessary release.

Though we can't force laughter into our lives, we can invite its restorative and healing properties into our way of doing things. That could simply mean allowing ourselves to smile and laugh out loud at a fond, somewhat hilarious, memory. Don't ignore a happy recollection just because it's in your past and has nothing to do with what you're doing right this second. Thinking back on something really funny can release you from what may be a much too serious moment. And we do take ourselves awfully seriously. More than we should. So much so that we forget how liberating a good laugh can be. Indeed, nurturing your sense of humor is putting laughter's antidotal powers to work.

Many years ago, as I entered the struggle of being a preadolescent daughter, a certain, funny ritual took hold in my house, a ritual that seemed to transcend the antagonism that muscled its way between me and my mother. Prior to the days of automatic garage-door openers, my mother and I employed a system of our own. About twenty minutes or so after I'd get home from school, my mother would pull into the driveway and, when she had groceries to unload, would toot the horn. That was my signal to open the garage door. I thought of this as just one more of my jobs around the house, like feeding the dog.

I'd go into the garage and then before lifting it up, I'd lower myself right below a row of windows that faced the driveway. Then, slowly, I'd stand up and suddenly my face would appear in one of those windows. Each and every time my mother broke into huge peals of laughter. I couldn't hear her mirth, but I knew from the expression on her face that for a few seconds we were sharing something completely inane. This effortless performance and the consistently positive reviews always gave me something to look forward to. To make someone laugh, to infuse something funny into her bloodstream, made me feel like a million bucks.

When our bloodstreams run with laughter, we become more receptive to the lighter side of life. Whether it's loud and raucous or quiet and reflective, laughter becomes a positive—and occasionally silly—filter through which we can see the world. Just as a meditative prayer can bring solace and peace, laughter, too, can soothe and soften. This is particularly true when we wear our laughter inside out. When we can laugh at ourselves—our sins, our obsessions, our tendency to be too serious—life seems a little more precious, a little less uncertain. So the next time you hear something funny, go ahead and laugh like there's no tomorrow. It's still good medicine, and I'm pretty sure it's what makes the world go round.

6 Collect Your Lucky Charms

"I've always thought you've got to believe in luck to get it."

—VICTORIA HOLT, *THE PRIDE OF THE PEACOCK* (1976)

A WHILE BACK I OPENED A BOOK to a page packed with dried, flattened four-leaf clovers. I'd written a date in the upper-right-hand corner: Saturday, May 31, 1980, a year away from college graduation. I don't recall where I picked the clovers, but discovering them inside the book reminded me of how much stock I put into anything that might possibly bring me good luck.

As a child, I honestly believed that God had given me the magnificent skill of finding pennies and four-leaf clovers just about anywhere but particularly in my neighbors' yards and driveways. Scooping up a shiny penny or spotting a four-leaf clover was as much a part of my childhood as hide-and-seek and playing with dolls. The funny thing is that as I got older, collecting pennies and clovers seemed silly, almost embarrassing. I still play hide-and-seek when I need a moment of refuge from my family—my closet works well. And, up until about two years ago, when my daughter's interest in Barbie began to wane, I did play with dolls.

Lately, though, I've renewed my belief in luck. And although I may turn around to see who's looking, I've begun to reach down for those pennies with greater frequency. They usually disappear into the bottomless pit of my pocketbook. But for me the collection is as valuable as having a few extra Band-Aids on hand.

By itself, luck is a gift without a giver or recipient. For luck to truly have some meaning, you must do something with it. Yet without believing in good fortune, it's not likely to make itself evident. That's why, as you collect your good luck charms, you must create tangible, it-can-happen dreams. Surrounding yourself with a few lucky charms is a lot like prayer. It's fortification for the unknown, a sort of spiritual coat of armor that can soften some of the blows in life and heighten and enhance the highs you never thought possible.

As children, we walked carefully. If you stepped on a crack, well, you knew what would happen. I don't think we were so afraid of the cracks as we were empowered by our ability to keep bad things from happening to our mothers' backs. Just the other day, as I walked across a parking lot with my seven-year-old friend Maddie, I was delighted as she described in intricate detail her strategy for keeping her feet from getting wet. "The yellow lines are the ocean," she explained as she took wide steps that led her to safety. Her movements—indeed her sense of control—made her feel safe.

For some people, their lucky charm is a strand of garlic or a kitchen witch hanging over a sink or hiding away in the pantry. It's nothing to be ashamed of. In fact, collecting and keeping our charms within easy reach can become constant reminders of what we value in life. Collecting charms also can take some of the pressure off. We can influence an awful lot in life, but, let's face it: much of what we're handed has nothing to do with what we've wished for, much less imagined in our wildest dreams or nightmares. When we add a few charms to our life-living arsenal, we spread out some of the hard work that goes into our day-to-day movements.

Your charm collection should be a reflection of who you are. And don't worry about keeping them all in one place. I have quotes I read weekly—one is on the refrigerator, a few are on my desk. Others float in and out of drawers. An old pair of early sixties–vintage sunglasses rests in an old printers box hanging on my bedroom wall.

As your collection grows, don't underestimate its worth on the open market. Just take a look at a friend's expression when you place one of your charms into his or her hand.

7 Linger in the Tub

"I can't think of any sorrow in the world that a hot bath [or shower] wouldn't help, just a little bit."

—SUSAN GLASPELL, *THE VISIONING* (1911)

SOMETIMES I FORGET TO WASH BEHIND MY EARS. But at the end of most days—especially if I've played in the dirt—I like nothing more than taking a hot, steamy shower. All it takes is an inexpensive mesh sponge and my favorite liquid body cleanser.

As a child, I distinctly remember bath time. "Let's wash behind your ears," my father or mother would say. I wondered then, as I do today, how dirt could possibly hide behind my ears. Yet like my parents before me, I make the same declaration to my six-year-old son, who miraculously sits still for this long-held custom. Perhaps in his mind there is a silent reference to something other than dirt. In any case, he allows this short interruption and then quickly returns to his own version of this popular relaxing ritual.

Aside from washing away the dirt and sweat that our bodies accumulate, the relaxing qualities associated with bathing are plentiful and, like a multivitamin, are packed with extraordinary therapeutic powers. Even the sound of water—either pulsating from a shower head or splashing in a bath—can settle a strong emotion and help you to loosen up for a few calming moments.

If you're willing to turn a bath or shower into a journey toward someplace calm and soothing, you're more likely to create an environment that truly comforts. Achieving a squeaky-clean exterior is all well and good. Sweating out your tension and becoming blissfully unaware of your troubles are even better. Dust off that aromatherapy candle and unwrap the scrumptiously scented soap you've been saving for a special occasion. Bring in the radio or play the music of your choice. You might even belt out a few numbers and pretend you're on that stage you've always dreamed of.

For some, a long soak or the chance to stand under the shower for more than a few minutes is simply more than they can imagine: too much to do, no privacy, and all that comes with a busy person's life. Yet the restorative benefits of bathing are really too good to pass up. As easy as it is to pamper others, many of us find it difficult—impossible even—to indulge ourselves. Taking a hot bath or shower is an easy exercise in self-care. It opens up your senses, strengthens your well-being, and renews your ability to nurture others.

As a mother, I have finally reached the point where a closed door usually stays that way unless I say "Come in" or I open it myself. My other trick is to simply keep my plan to myself. Once, when I had the house to myself, I even set up a lovely bath in the middle of the day, in the middle of the week. It's become one of those memories that lingers with a pleasure not unlike the memory of a favorite dessert, the taste of which can be conjured up years later.

Giving your inhibitions a respite is another good reason to immerse yourself in warm water. Whether it's a bubbling Jacuzzi or an old, claw-footed tub, few places can offer the safety and freedom of a bath. Sometimes I stand outside the bathroom door when my kids are bathing. I might hear my son, who's lying flat on his stomach (sometimes I sneak a peek), orchestrating the interaction between the hottest action figure and something with more history, like a rubber duck. Listening to my eleven-year-old daughter provides an unplugged concert of selected top-forty hits. For a little while, at the end of the day, *they're* in charge. One's a director. The other, a star.

Last night, after the director and star were in bed, I ran the water for a bath. As I reached for some towels from the linen closet, my daughter called out from her room, "*You're* taking a bath?" "Yes," I replied, "*I'm* taking a bath." The nerve, right? Well, a few minutes later, I removed the sack of toys that usually hangs in the bath, and I gingerly stepped into the bubble-filled tub. And although I didn't sing or wash behind my ears, I did manage to read some great literature—the Crate and Barrel catalog—from cover to cover. I'd walked right through heaven's door and furnished my entire house—in my dreams, anyway.

A Pantry for Your Bath

A shelf, a drawer, or a basket can be the perfect place to store your bathing essentials. Collect your favorite fragrant oils, bath salts, and sponges, and remember to use them when you're in the mood for luxury. If you travel, slip these accoutrements into your suitcase. My friend Chris has no qualms about taking her bath on the road. For her, it makes the business of traveling on the job a little calmer, a little less hectic, and a touch more pampering.

8 Talk Back

"I believe in a lively disrespect for most forms of authority."
—Rita Mae Brown, *Starting from Scratch* (1988)

One of the toughest lessons in childhood is learning when to keep our mouths shut. As a kid, I talked back a lot, and I got into a lot of trouble. Naturally, I grew up associating my apparent insolence with life's more negative outcomes.

It wasn't until I grew up and began witnessing my own children's penchant for talking back that I realized some of the character-building potential that talking back can offer. It's no surprise that their expressions sharply remind me of my own days of getting in the last word. I decided long ago, though, that as a parent it is my job to channel my kids' headstrong ways into a tenacious spirit that will carry them over all the hurdles that lay before them.

More than three centuries have passed since Anne Bradstreet wrote in *Meditations Divine and Moral*, "Authority without wisdom is like a heavy axe without an edge, fitter to bruise than polish," but the meaning of those words is as true today as it was then. Allowing yourself to question authority is the first step toward learning how to talk back with grace and diplomacy. Indeed, too much authority is without wisdom, and if you can't learn something from it (or teach something to others), then authority really has no substance.

In some cases, talking back means not talking at all; you simply proceed without hesitation. Sometimes the authoritative voice comes from within: "You can't do that!" you say to yourself. Other times authority is a direct edict from someone who's lived so long by the rules she or he can't imagine a life without them: "You can't go there!" someone might say as you walk through a door anyway.

If you can eliminate your fear of negative outcomes and concentrate, instead, upon your right to be heard, talking back can lead to wonderful discoveries about yourself and the world around you. When we talk back, we stand up for ourselves and make ourselves count. Even if you don't get exactly what you want, you're sending a clear message that says, "My opinion matters." And maybe, just maybe, your opinion will find its way into a new policy or change someone's narrow point of view.

When we disassociate talking back with words like *impertinent* and *disrespect*, we make more room for expressions that suggest strength, creativity, and courage. When we stifle our need to speak out, we create a place for resentment. Later, we might berate ourselves for keeping quiet, for choosing the status quo. In many cases, though, it's better—and more honest—to talk back. If you are feeling a little unsure, frame your assertiveness in a question. For example, instead of saying, "No, I'm not going to do it that way," gently ask, "Is it possible for us to approach this from another direction?"

The risk of backing down versus talking back can have lifelong consequences. For example, if you supress an objection to something close to your heart—something that really matters—you may lose a piece of yourself. Think of the number of times you've kicked yourself for not speaking up and spent way too much time regretting your silence. It's true that some people thrive on controversy. Yet others shrink from it. You can take the middle road *and* stand up for yourself by *carefully* choosing what's important.

As children, many of us had a hard time standing up for ourselves. When we did talk back, our opinions weren't always validated, and sometimes the risks were great. But talking back helped us grow up. It also reinforced our inner voice.

Though archaic by most standards, the notion that children should be seen and not heard still runs through our collective psyches. And although many of us have moved away from this form of childrearing, we occasionally may slip into that childlike frame of mind that warns us to keep our points of view to ourselves. Yet how refreshing to see a little girl stand up for what she believes! How victorious for a child to stand six feet tall just for speaking his mind! The lesson here is timeless and reminds us that the spirit that drove us to talk back as kids is as powerful now as it was then.

How hard can it be to speak your mind? Well, depending on where you're sitting, it can be risky. If your audience isn't prepared to listen, you can be fairly certain you won't be heard. Your opinion may not garner the respect you think it deserves. You may actually surprise someone with your boldness, forever changing a relationship. In short, you need to be prepared for the consequences. Your silence, on the other hand, has consequences as well.

Generally speaking, it's still a good idea to listen more than we talk. Yet if you constantly quell your need to talk back, you deny yourself the chance to grow and ultimately to change. And without change, you're likely to miss half the fun.

9 "Be My Valentine"

"Love is a fruit in season at all times."

—MOTHER TERESA, *A GIFT FOR GOD* (1975)

IN FEBRUARY, LOVE IS IN THE AIR. Maybe you wear red and bring heart-shaped cookies into work. Perhaps you celebrate with a box of chocolates and a glass of champagne. If you're creative, you might make cards out of paper doilies and silver and gold glitter. But who says you have to wait until Valentine's Day to celebrate matters of the heart? After all, it's always nice to hear that you're loved, no matter what day it is.

Still, most of us received intense training. Starting at an early age, many of us exchanged cards, even with kids we hardly knew or—worse—with kids we didn't like. Whether you made yours from scratch or bought them at the store, it was easy to be swept up into everything red and pink. The small envelopes and the extra cards for teachers had me hooked for years. And more than any other homework assignment, the task of creating my own personal valentine box was as close to arts and crafts heaven as I've ever come.

After finding an empty shoebox, I'd pull together the essentials—tin foil, paper, scraps of felt, glue, and scissors. I marveled at how easily the foil attached itself to the box and its miraculous metamorphosis from something utilitarian—a cover-up for leftovers—into something shiny and decorative. Carrying home the box, stuffed with cards and scattered candy hearts, made me feel like royalty, like I was part of a huge celebratory procession.

That's probably what's most appealing about this holiday: it is so easy to make someone else feel good. Eleven years ago, I'd just given birth to my daughter. I was out of sync with Cupid and all other objects related to Valentine's Day, though completely delighted to accept a delivery of flowers from my husband. "To the loves of my life," said the card, which I read out loud over and over. I wanted this week-old baby to know that she was the love of someone's life and that even in the tired lives of a new mother and child, celebrations were still possible. Those flowers stood on the bureau until the petals fell and the leaves grew crisp. It was hard to throw them away.

You can say "I love you" in a number of ways. An out-of-the-blue card with a message like "Thinking of you" speaks volumes about your affection. Buy a small gift for a friend feeling sad. If you've had a disagreement, be the first to wave the white flag. Ignore your pride and apologize. Or pick up the phone and remind someone who loves you that the feeling is mutual. Make your declarations of love a part of your everyday life. Listen, too, as others make declarations to you.

Two of my oldest and dearest friends have my heart in common. They don't know each other, but both have stayed with me through the best and worst of times. Throughout the years, we've maintained ties mostly by telephone. At the end of each conversation, I hear these words: "I love you." For many years, I'd mumble something back like, "Thanks," or "Me, too." I didn't know where to put their words, yet after each good-bye my heart grew, and I finally discovered where the words found a place. Now, I am the first to say "I love you" to them, straight from my heart.

Declaring your love on Valentine's Day is a lovely way to remind others that you hold them in your heart. But doing so on any other day is just as sweet—and that pound of chocolate will never be turned away! But the thirsty heart is

The feeling is mutual

not that easy to quench. Indeed, if we're lucky, our thirst for love is lifelong. Similarly, our capacity to love is infinite. No one knows how much a heart can hold. When you fill someone's heart—regardless of the day—you're not depleting your own. The love in your heart is regenerative; as soon as you let some go, you get back an equal dose and sometimes more.

Say It from the Heart

Write the words below on small pieces of paper. Then fold up the papers, place them in a jar, and, once in awhile, declare your love by mailing one to a friend or family member. They'll be happy to hear from you and even more delighted to know they reside in your heart.

I love you.	Hooray for you!	You're the best.
You're dear.	You're special.	You're beautiful.
Hug me.	E-mail me.	You make me laugh.
Call me.	You're precious.	You mean a lot to me.
I miss you.	You mean the world	You brighten my day.
You're wonderful.	to me.	You are my friend.

10 Stand Up and Cheer

"A little praise is not only merest justice but is beyond the purse of no one."
—EMILY POST, *ETIQUETTE* (1922)

WHEN I DESCRIBED THE CONCEPT OF THIS BOOK to my old friend Robin, she implored me to include a chapter on clapping. "Applause! Applause!" she exclaimed, immediately reminding me of our school days, when, at the drop of a hat, Robin would throw her hands together in celebration of someone's (including her own) good fortune. The memory resurfaced so quickly and with such fondness that for a moment I felt that adolescent joy all over again.

Some of my best days were spent at Robin's house, mostly in the kitchen, where we swirled around with her sisters talking about school, boys, and what we might find in the refrigerator. In her kitchen and elsewhere, Robin didn't hold back her enthusiasm for some of our most minor triumphs. I can still hear her impromptu cheers of support. Even today, as a social worker, Robin employs her clapping strategy in her work. "If someone achieves 100 days of sobriety, we celebrate," she says.

Cheering for others accentuates life's important events. Often, a round of applause is preceded by a split second of silence—the pause that separates a wonderful performance from the praise it deserves. The silence enables us to gather our strength and enthusiasm that moments later thunder through the roar of applause.

Children are particularly good at filling a room with praise. And although some kids are more reserved than others, together they exude a contagious sense of unconditional support. They also love to celebrate just about anything, spontaneously moving, shaking, and clapping when good things are in the air. Eventually the clapping and celebrating comes full circle, with everyone feeling a little better about themselves. When kids cheer for their friends, they feel connected and part of a group. They also begin to imagine how it must feel to be admired and praised—a wonderful thrill.

Giving applause also signifies approval. The child who takes her first steps is greeted with rounds of applause. For the parents, it is a joyful moment, complete with smiles and sometimes even tears. Sensing everyone's joy, the child understands that it is her actions that have brought smiles to the faces around her. As she takes another step, more smiles spill forth, and the cycle begins again. Front-row seats at an encore performance. It doesn't get much better.

In a more formal setting, like a wedding or an awards ceremony, applause may be the preferred form of expression. Language suddenly becomes woefully inadequate and somehow out of place. Rules of protocol no longer apply. Only something bigger than words will suffice. Not surprisingly, the applause grows a little louder when we're clapping for someone we love.

Clapping, accompanied by some hearty cheering, can also be an expression of empathy. Sometimes we really do know how good it feels to do something right, to win an accolade, to succeed. Applauding a friend's victory—a triumph that might parallel one of your own—sends a genuine message that says, "I understand the joy you're feeling and I'm thrilled for you!" These declarations of support further remind us of our own inner strength, our energy, and our ability to hold *ourselves* up under pressure. Standing on the sidelines and watching each play certainly gives us a grand perspective. Yet if we can understand the plays as well, even step into the game once in a while, we're in a much better position to be an advocate.

Clapping for our loved ones is also a healthy and productive way to step away from ourselves. We get so bogged down in our own personal rat race. We forget that we've got lots of company on the race course, people just like us. People who could use a "Nice going!" or a "Way to go!" once in a while. Don't think of your expressions of support as gestures you might have saved for yourself. Praise is like love: the more you give, the more you get. In fact, if you do take a little time to praise others, you're more likely to be on the receiving end of a similar exchange. But don't wait for reciprocity to kick in; offer praise and support because someone deserves it and will feel better because of it. Watching others as they stand in the limelight shows us how we can effectively enjoy our own success—an invaluable and instructive course in living.

So, as you move from day to day, consider the ways in which you might support those within your circle. Friends, family, and colleagues can all benefit from your praise. If you are especially at a loss for words and something truly extraordinary is in the air, then for a small moment rely on the universal language of applause. Your message will be heard loud and clear.

11 Give Yourself a Gold Star

"There is an applause superior to that of the multitude—one's own."
—Elizabeth Elton Smith, *The Three Eras of Woman's Life* (1836)

Close your eyes and imagine those small gold stars stuck to the top corners of your first-grade papers. Didn't you love getting those stars? It was like being the sheriff of arithmetic or spelling. A star meant that your efforts had paid off.

Of course, it was easy to accept those symbols of achievement, especially because they came from someone most of us wanted to please. As we grow older, though, the gold stars lose some of their potency. It takes more than a sticker to get us motivated. Grades replace stickers, and, later, when we go to work, report cards become performance evaluations. But somehow these external kudos—the acclaim we seek from the outside—aren't enough.

That's why it's important to give yourself a gold star. Recognizing your achievements—big and small—is an important part of honoring who you are. Gold stars have the powerful effect of undermining and dethroning all the critical stuff you've heard about yourself. I'm constantly shutting out the sounds of my own voice telling me I've done something wrong, something irreconcilable. If I can respond with something positive—something that I've done right—I'm a winner. If I succumb to the negative banter, I lose every time.

Several months ago I clipped a list of phrases that came home from my daughter's school—parenting Cliff Notes that are securely taped on the cabinet next to my kitchen sink. "Congratulations! You got it right!" "You must have been secretly practicing." I love that one. "You've really mastered that!" Every so often I glance up while I'm washing the dishes and read one of those lines to myself. It's one small way of giving myself a gold star. I should probably do this with more regularity. But it's not always as easy as reading a list.

Sometimes giving yourself a gold star seems terribly uncomfortable and even a little self-serving. Yet affirming your self-worth is one of the best ways you can treat yourself to what really matters. If you're good at praising others but minimize your own accomplishments—big and small—pay closer attention to the way people react to your praise. Notice their delight and then, later, practice on yourself.

You can give yourself a gold star first by paying close attention to the good things you do. Don't let them slide by unnoticed. Tell a trusted friend that you got through a difficult time. Buy yourself a special gift. You can write your gold stars into a journal, describing what you accomplished and how good it made you feel. Give yourself a hug—literally! Cross your arms over your heart and hold yourself for a few seconds; it's a physical reminder that you have yourself to love.

Like children, we flourish under the benefits of encouragement, praise, approval, and acceptance. If we live with encouragement—especially our own—we learn to be confident. If we live with self-praise, we learn to appreciate what's around us. If we coexist with self-approval, we're more likely to give ourselves—and others—a little slack. If we accept our good deeds, we're inclined to be more open to the good in the world around us.

Sometimes I give myself a gold star for simply getting through the mass hysteria that occasionally descends upon our household as we try to get a start on the day. If someone is getting on your nerves and it's not even nine in the morning, give yourself a gold star. A doughnut and a cup of coffee, a quick walk outside if it's a nice day. It's not always easy to remember to give yourself a gold star. If this is the case with you, buy some gold stickers like the ones given out in school. Stick them on your computer screen. Put one in the corner of your bathroom mirror or in the middle of your steering wheel. Think of these stars like a piece of string tied to your finger—subtle reminders of your major and minor accomplishments.

Gold-Star Shorthand

Write these phrases down—or make up your own—and post them where you'll see them frequently. Say them out loud. Say them to yourself and to others. Just make sure you say them.

Congratulations! You got it right!

Now that is what I call a great job.

You must have been secretly practicing.

That was first-class work.

I knew you could do it!

That's the best ever.

I am proud of the work you did today.

You have really mastered that!

You are on the right track.

You're a winner.

12 Do One Thing at a Time

"She moved with a slowness that was a sign of richness; cream does not pour quickly."

—Rebecca West, *Black Lamb and Grey Falcon* (1941)

A FEW MONTHS AGO I stood at the front desk of my doctor's office about to schedule another appointment. Not wanting to waste any time, I flipped through my day planner, jotting notes here and there as if I were back in school. As the man standing next to me watched, he finally said, "Multitasking?" "Yes," I said, "always."

I used to like that nineties term coined to describe a person's superhuman abilities to juggle and wear numerous hats. Yet as time goes on, I've come to have a love-hate relationship with my ability to do three things at once. Sometimes, particularly as I'm preparing dinner, I don't know what to do next. Maybe it's because I think of doing things in groups—what can I clean, put away, and cook all at the same time? And can I do any of it well?

I remember years ago asking my sister if she ever felt overwhelmed just by looking at her kitchen counter. "All the time," she answered. I felt better but somehow bothered, too, that something so mundane as a kitchen counter could produce such stress.

Recently, though, I've begun to slow down and do things one at a time. I'm inspired—and simultaneously exasperated—by my son, who, like most six-year-olds, likes to take his time to get to where he wants to be. It's as if he truly savors the path more than the destination. As I prod him to "hurry up," he slows down to relish his journey even more. His way, I'm sure, of subtly telling me who's in control.

I worry a lot that my rushing around is rubbing off on my children in ways that may prevent them from living and enjoying their moments. It's easy, even attractive, to be part of a whirlwind schedule. Yet it feels wrong to burden my family with a pace that seems to wear everyone out. Occasionally, someone will bring my crimes out in the open. "You always rush me!" says my daughter. "I hate that!" When I hear those words, I want to crawl away. Naturally, when I'm the one running late, I hear my words hurled back in my direction. When I add, "It's not the end of the world if we're a little late," my credibility is practically nonexistent and flimsy at best.

Rushing and doing too many things at once can be one of the greatest stressors in life. Promise yourself to be more single-minded in your movements, and you're likely to experience a calmness that's almost immediate. If, like me, you're overwhelmed by a kitchen counter filled to the brim, look at what you see with a slow and steady eye—a carton of milk that needs to be put away, some vegetable scraps to be scooped up and saved for the compost. In a few minutes, your counter is clear. And so is your head. Instead of doing things all at once, slow down and do one thing at a time. You'll be surprised at how quickly your task is done.

It's unrealistic to think that we can stop like a small child to examine what's happening around us. Commitments and, yes, burdensome schedules are all part of being grown up. Yet a child's ability to focus on the minutia is something to admire and borrow from time to time. Clearly, a preschooler isn't thinking about deadlines, mortgages, or what he's going to prepare the family for dinner. And those things don't go away just because you don't want to think about them. However, slowing down and occasionally doing one thing at a time won't make your adult concerns any bigger than they already are. In fact, with a little perspective, those concerns might even become smaller and more manageable.

When we move more slowly, our lives have a chance of becoming less of a blur. Our moments may even begin to stand out and then burrow into our memories to be conjured up again and again. For me, one of those moments occurred far away from home. Many years ago, at the age of seventeen, I spent a summer in Kenya. I was an exchange student living with a family in Nairobi. At one point, I left with a friend to visit the bush country. No running water, outhouses with leaves where you'd expect a roll of toilet paper, and children who rubbed my skin to find my true color.

One day my friend and I hiked up a small mountain, and once we reached the top, I knew that the scene before me would never leave my mind's eye. The lush, green stillness—except for the smoke that rose out of the huts below—has stayed with me. I didn't rush this moment. Indeed, I could hardly bear the thought that it would end. But I knew it would, so I stared for a long time. I have a photograph, but that one thing—just absorbing what I could in the time that I had—is what I cherish the most about that summer.

As you begin to do things one at a time, pay attention to the way you interact with your surroundings. You're likely to become more receptive to what life has to offer. Plus, you'll enhance your ability to listen more carefully to what people are saying. You'll get a broader view of the world and minimize the risks of missing the things that really matter, the things that often are the most fun.

13 Don't Get Ready, Don't Get Set—Just Go

"The cream of enjoyment in this life is always impromptu. The chance walk; the unexpected visit; the unpremeditated journey; the unsought conversation or acquaintance."

—FANNY FERN, *CAPER SAUCE* (1872)

MY FRIENDS ED AND DONNA have enviable parenting skills. Every so often, one of them issues this rousing clarion call: "Pajama run!" It's a family ritual, one their two daughters know well. Donned in sleepwear, toward the tail end of the witching hour, the kids are whisked away into the night for a spontaneous ice cream treat.

Though they've woven this tradition into their lives like a richly patterned tapestry, Ed and Donna have still managed to infuse this beloved activity with a spur-of-the-moment spirit. Their ability and willingness to embrace spontaneity not only enhances the family's together time, but also demonstrates their belief that good things can be pulled out of thin air. This is especially remarkable when the good things—indeed, the good times—appear on no one's schedule but their own.

Sometimes, though, we grown-ups have a tough time with unplanned events. Somewhere along the way, we lose our childlike tendencies to accept the unexpected, to dispense with worry, and to infuse surprise and serendipity into our lives. It's as if we've seen way too many rabbits come out of black hats. Yet no one ever said kids have the market on spontaneity. Indeed, we can learn from the ease with which children put aside one thing for something better, something that appears out of nowhere. From a wide-eyed expression to an enthusiastic "Wow!" a child knows the worth of life's unforeseen treasures: the extra half hour outside on a particularly beautiful night, the let's-go-right-now trip to the beach, the last-minute lemonade stand that pulls in five bucks.

Anticipating something wonderful has its own kind of thrill. Looking forward to a long-planned vacation. The meticulous selection of a special gift for a special friend. Awaiting the birth of your first child or the moment when an adoption becomes final. Somehow the joy is magnified—doubled really—when, after the anticipation, something wonderful happens, something truly worth the wait.

But when a thrill unexpectedly drops out of the sky, well, it's almost a sign from somewhere ethereal to start jumping up and down or, at the very least, to prevent yourself from having second thoughts. Enjoying life in an out-of-the-blue sort of way can be the perfect antidote to the rigidity that so often constricts our carefully planned movements. Too often, we mistake spontaneity for wastefulness or a sense of whimsy for silliness. Embracing spontaneity is good exercise for the creative spirit, which, like a well-toned muscle, becomes stronger and stronger over time.

A popular writing exercise is a good example. In many workshops, the instructor will talk some and then ask the class to whip out a piece of paper and just start writing. Participants are dumbfounded: What?! Just like that? The activity is intended to strip everyone of her or his inhibitions and worries regarding the written word. Very likely you've paid a fee to attend, and, naturally, you're motivated to give it a try. Yet beyond the financial incentive, the few minutes you spend composing really can enhance your ability to create, to shut out the negativism and plunge forward with whatever's on your mind.

In many ways, spontaneity is synonomous with creativity. When you lose the ability to be spontaneous, you risk losing your creative drive. In the workplace, managers may turn to toys and play to engender a creative environment. Often, the idea is to divert people's attention from standard operating procedures—policies that keep things running smoothly yet limit the imagination.

Some people, especially policy lovers, are afraid of spontaneity. Something bad might happen. They might not be prepared. But for what? Even if it's written down in ink and copied 100,000 times for distribution, things change. In more ways then we probably realize, change and our response to it can dress up our creative spirit. Change tests our ability and willingness to be flexible and see things in ways that, in the end, can enrich our lives.

Ultimately, all the planning and organizing and time managing can never replace what we learn when we let life just happen. A lot of life's pleasures and once-in-a-lifetime experiences happen whether you write them down or not, whether they're planned for or appear out of a black hat. So, from time to time, leave your schedule behind. After all, the unplanned moments—the ones we can't rehearse—are very often the richest.

Spontaneity 101

If you're a little rusty in the areas of surprise and spontaneity, try the following:

- Next time you get the urge to do something outrageous, give in and do it.
- If you pick up but then put down a book at the bookstore, decide to buy it.
- Watch a late movie tonight.
- Bring two brown-bag lunches to a friend's house.
- Call an old friend.
- Write a letter to the editor of your local paper.
- Part your hair on the other side.
- See if you can still do fifty sit-ups.
- Buy a helium balloon and tie it outside your front door.
- Eat cereal for dinner . . . and ice cream for breakfast.

14 Sing at the Top of Your Lungs

"Let your soul do the singin'."

—MA RAINEY, TO BESSIE SMITH, IN STUDS TERKEL, *GIANTS OF JAZZ* (1957)

I DON'T SING IN THE CAR, which is why I sing in the shower. I used to sing in the car until the familiar voices behind me moaned in unison, "Mom, stop!" Once in a while, though, I forget the protocol and actually belt out one-sixteenth of a song. But I get heckled every time, especially if I make up my own lyrics. Still, I'm trying to teach my kids that it's OK for *everyone* to sing in the car, so I listen with pleasure as they mimic the latest stars of teen pop. So far, though, this object lesson hasn't taken hold.

Nonetheless, the sound of their uninhibited voices is, well, music to my ears. Whether they're performing backup for the hottest new act or, with their friends, entertaining dinner guests à la karaoke, the music they create is one of the purest forms of joy I can think of. Sometimes I can't even hear the radio. But that's OK, because in a few short years, when I'm by myself in the car, the sound of the radio will stir echoes of that singing, and I'll miss it so much.

When you're very young, you don't care how your voice sounds. You just want to be loud. You're certainly not worried about what people think. It's those older people singing off-key that catches *your* attention. When kids sing, they're in Carnegie Hall, whether outside on the playground, in the church or synagogue choir, or in the shower.

Sometimes kids sing to improve their situations. One friend tells the story of her younger sister, who turned to music whenever she felt excluded. Outside, for instance, she'd hop on her bike and, at the top of her lungs, sing one spiritual after the other. "She'd sing 'Michael Row the Boat Ashore' and 'Kumbaya,' always getting our attention and always making us laugh." Today, like her sister did years ago, my friend relies on the soothing powers of music. In her car is a stack of "favorite sing-along compact discs," which she plays during her commute to and from work. "I'm sure I look hilarious," she says, "but it winds me down and makes driving through rush hour a little less tense."

During a recent annual checkup, my daughter unexpectedly broke into song just as the nurse jabbed a needle into her arm. Instead of the usual crying that one hears in a doctor's office, on that day patients and their parents heard something a little different. I was thrilled that my little diva could relieve some of her tension by creating a beautiful sound. I don't know if she was truly aware of what was happening as she sang. It didn't matter, though. In those few seconds, my daughter worked through a typical, though traumatic, childhood experience. Shots are no fun, but if singing can minimize the agony, then perhaps the anticipation of the next injection won't be fraught with such fear and dread.

Hearing yourself sing—whether you're singing into a microphone, a hairbrush, or a wooden spoon—can unravel your mysteries and clarify what's running back and forth between your head and heart. Hearing the sound of your own voice, especially when it's surrounded by a familiar and supportive chorus (at a religious service, for instance), is also a powerful reminder of everyone's creative spirit. Indeed, singing helps us *find* our voice.

I still love cranking up the volume on the stereo until I think the house is shaking. And even though the music drowns out my own efforts—a good thing if my kids are present—I revel in the exhilaration that comes from filling my lungs with that perfect combination of melody and oxygen.

Playing music is also cathartic. My friend Bill has played guitar and piano for years. He's a father of three and works a lot of hours. But whenever he can, he plays his music. He has about five guitars in his basement, but it's the one he keeps in his office that gives new meaning to work-life balance. Occasionally, harmonica player Little Arthur Duncan, a local Chicago legend, will stop by to jam with Bill. For Bill, it's a kick and a great release. For his customers and employees, it's an unexpected and enviable thrill—one that a lot of us could use in the middle of our workdays.

Remember, though, that the human voice—your voice—is really the finest musical instrument there is. It's your breath, your energy, your expression. What's most remarkable is its portability—wherever you go, your capacity to sing follows. When I was a young girl, I must have sung *something* every day. Summer camp especially provided a musical springboard for everyone. We'd sing on our way to dinner, we'd sing through dinner, we'd sing anywhere. I'll never forget one particularly warm afternoon when a thunderstorm seduced our entire cabin into washing our hair under the pouring rain. Imagine a dozen teenage girls dancing on a mountain, singing "I'm Gonna Wash That Man Right out of My Hair." Not exactly *South Pacific* but still an image that is emblazoned in my memory and one that consistently brings an enormous grin to my heart.

15 Stay Up Past Your Bedtime

"There's a big moon shining down on us.

Let's go out tonight.

Let's go out tonight."

—BRUCE HENDERSON, "BIG MOON" (1997)

ONE OF MY MOST VISCERAL CHILDHOOD MEMORIES is the adrenaline rush I experienced each time I realized I'd been playing outside too long. Somebody would be called in to dinner or, finally, I'd look up into the sky and notice, with some alarm, that it was much later than I had thought.

Eventually, my parents gave me a watch. Instead of waiting until my friends had disappeared into their houses or relying on the sun's steady fall, I began to tell myself the time, which was not always on my side. But the watch's usefulness didn't last. I still wanted more time outside. So I began to set the watch back about ten minutes every night. My trick worked for a while but not long enough. Yet even at the age of eight I'd begun the sneaky business of breaking my own curfew.

When we were teenagers, curfews curtailed our nightlife (that, of course, was the idea). As we grew older, though, we worried less about coming home on time and more about getting enough sleep. Staying up past our bedtimes became less of a sport and more just another part of our adult lives. For many of us, our bedtimes are sacred. After all, we're always rushing everywhere—to our jobs, to the store, to the train, to the gym. No wonder we can't stay up late anymore. But once in awhile, it's fun to push yourself beyond your normal limit, especially if you can tack on an extra hour of sleep in the morning.

When you stay up past your bedtime, you open yourself up for more: like the tail end of a really important conversation ("Oh, I can stay a few more minutes"), the long list of credits of a really good movie ("I *knew* she was the one who sang that song"), or the nothing-can-compare sunset that you've always wanted to see.

Staying up past your bedtime is ultimately about giving yourself more freedom. When you allow yourself to linger—anywhere—you're telling yourself that it's OK to defy not only time itself, but the restrictive nature of time that leads you frantically from one activity to another. When we tie ourselves down with crazy schedules, we give away our freedom. And every time we chip away at our freedom, we feed our habit to always be *doing*. Ask anyone, especially yourself, if this feels healthy, if this is what really matters.

Breaking our own curfews also speaks of our willingness to be accountable. Clearly, when you break your curfew, you may face a few consequences—temporary fatigue, for instance, or the need to apologize for not making a promised phone call. But consequences are usually manageable. Indeed, sometimes you *can* have your cake and eat it, too. You just might have to postpone the feast or have only a nibble here and there. Yes, you need to get your sleep, and yes, you're not usually out so late, but, hey, taking a few extra minutes at the end of your day might be the perfect reminder that your life is your own.

Night Life

Consider staying up past your bedtime for these reasons:

- You're reading a really good book.
- You're watching an excellent movie.
- The stars are out in full regalia.
- You're visiting a friend.
- The house is so quiet you just want to revel in the silence.
- You're at a fabulous party.
- You've almost made contact with Mr. or Ms. Right.

16 Stop, Look, and Listen

"Patience! Patience! Patience is the invention of dullards and sluggards. In a well-regulated world, there should be no need of such a thing as patience."
—GRACE KING, *BALCONY STORIES* (1892)

ON THE AFTERNOON OF HER FORTIETH BIRTHDAY, I called a friend to wish her well. I asked about her plans for the rest of the day and learned that a celebration had already taken place. In the morning, my friend, her two sisters, and her husband had risen high into the Kentucky sky in a hot-air balloon. "What was it like?" I asked. "Well, I don't know if I can explain it," she said. "I was so focused on the moment, when it was actually happening."

What I learned from my friend that morning is that sometimes, to be in the moment, you must surrender to it completely. That's not to say you won't remember it later, though you may forfeit the chance to put the moment into words. And although I couldn't say exactly what my pal experienced that morning, I heard the thrill and awe in her voice.

To truly be present, one must live *inside* the moment and experience it for its own sake. If you live *outside* the moment—observing and explaining—you're no longer absorbing and feeling. The moment breaks apart and eventually disappears. Think of a movie. Sometimes it's impossible to explain what you've seen. In some cases, you might still be processing what you saw. On another level, though, one you can't necessarily pinpoint, you know that once you begin dissecting your experience, you take away from it as well.

When you live inside the moment, you break ties with the past and the future. You put aside yesterday's regrets and shelve the fears of tomorrow, because ultimately these moments have minds of their own. And like sand through your fingertips, moments can't be held for long. Even if you only have them by a thread, your moments are worth holding on to, especially when you put them all together. After all, isn't a succession of moments what our lives are all about?

As hard as we try to hold onto our moments—recognizing and honoring them—it's still tempting, habitual really, to let them go, to minimize their presence. Instead of collecting them, we scatter our moments like marbles that roll in every direction. It reminds me of that old game, Hot Potato. Get rid of it, quick! It's as if we don't know what to do with the moment, as if we really have to do *something* with it.

Perhaps our penchant for minimizing the moment has something to do with waiting. As children, many of us learned exceedingly well how to wait. Wait until you're older, wait until you're bigger, wait until you finish your homework, wait until after school, wait until after dinner. We were told to wait a lot. So we waited, and instead of enjoying the moment, we focused on what we were waiting for. It's not surprising then that we tend to downgrade the moment or miss it altogether.

As I get older, the moment has become increasingly more important. When I yield to the moment, I stop fretting and worrying about the future. I stop guessing at what may happen and, instead, pay attention to what's right before my eyes. Sometimes the moment exhilarates like a bright and unexpected shooting star. Other times, the moment is painful, as if I'm getting poked repeatedly in the side.

A few years ago, I sat on my son's bedroom floor folding some baby clothes that he'd outgrown. I could feel the sadness and regret creeping in, but I wanted so badly to feel OK about the passage of time. I quickened my pace to push the pain away. I wanted the moment to be over. Suddenly, though, I looked up and noticed a very blue sky staring down through the window. Just feel it, I said to myself, as I slowed down, trying to focus on the task in front of me. I held a shirt close to my face and inhaled as deeply as I could. My heart seemed to crack and fill up at the same time as feelings of hope and loss collided right there in a pile of a little boy's old clothes. When I finally got up to leave the room, I wasn't sad anymore. Instead, I thought about the miraculous growth of a child, whose shirt size is less about loss and more about the gift of life itself.

I don't know if you can live inside each and every moment. But when you can, try to stop, look, and listen long enough to be right where you are, not in your past, not in your future. Just right in the middle of a split second in time.

17 Keep Your Eyes on Your Own Paper

"If what I am watching evaporated before my eyes, I would remain."
—ANNE TRUITT, *DAYBOOK* (1982)

IN HIGH SCHOOL, I had an evil biology teacher who once played a horrid little prank during a test. Our desks were arranged in exam position—military-like rows with evenly spaced room between each student. In the middle of the test, as my teacher walked up and down the aisles, he approached my desk and scooped up my paper. In the next instant I heard the sound of paper ripping and watched in horror as my classmates thought the worst. Oh, no, I thought; he thinks I was cheating! I wasn't, but maybe, somehow, I did look over at someone else's paper by accident. Oh, my God.

A few seconds later he returned the exam—intact—to my desk. "Just kidding," he said, holding in his other hand two torn sheets of paper. I told him I didn't think he was very funny, though to this day I think that in his own twisted way he was trying to tell us how he felt about cheating.

In school, the consequences of looking beyond your own desk were fairly tangible. An unconditional F was standard. Or maybe you'd have tea with the principal or, worse, the assistant principal, who lived for the likes of cheaters, slackers, and all-around troublemakers. I didn't know many cheaters then, and I can't think of anyone in my life today I'd consider a cheater in the traditional sense.

Yet in many ways, all of us are guilty at some point of cheating *ourselves.* I remember hearing that sentiment in school, but it wasn't until I'd grown up that I realized what they were talking about. For example, in these days of haves, have-nots, and those in between, we occasionally forget to keep our eyes on our own papers. Instead of focusing on what we do have, we look around and notice what others have, forgetting about our own good fortune.

Our tendency to pay attention to what other people are doing and what they have goes even deeper. If you don't keep your eyes on your own paper, you risk losing a piece of yourself. It's not cheating in the conventional sense, but it is a form of fraud none-theless. In the past, I was terribly guilty of asking others for their opinions, then scrambling them together like a huge everything-in-it Sunday morning omelet to come up with my own conclusion. Not surprisingly, my self-confidence suffered.

Back in school, many of us believed that the scribbles of our fellow pupils were somehow better, more accurate than what could possibly come from our own heads. Unfortunately, we may carry some of those same feelings into adulthood. Yet when we're too wrapped up in getting something right, we diminish the learning process and we diminish ourselves. Further, if we're always incor-porating other people's points of view, we tend to suppress our own ideas, our own ways of looking at things. And that can leave us feeling empty inside.

When we keep our eyes on our own papers, we live much closer to the truth, most of the time anyway. I think that's what our teachers were after so many years ago. We may not have heard the words *authentic* or *self-acceptance* when we were young, but, in many ways, that is what was, and still is, at stake. In the end, it is often more fruitful to look as deep inside as you can to find not necessarily the specific answer you're looking for but simply an answer. Only then can you begin to trust your instincts and, hopefully, accept who you are. Ultimately, it's all about choices, particularly the choice to honor yourself.

Accepting who you are can be as simple as refraining from asking others what they think of your new hairdo. Also, if you keep your eyes on your own paper, you're less likely to lose your focus. This is especially important if you're trying something new, working on your dreams, or shifting directions.

When you make the decision to look at your own paper—your own life and the way you think about it—you do something courageous. You dare to be yourself. It may be terrifying to search inward, particularly when it's so easy to look over someone else's shoulder. After all, when you peer inside, when you keep your eyes on your own paper, it's hard to know if you've made the correct choice. What if the answers are wrong? What if you don't know enough? But even if someone else's answers are right, they might not be right for you. Making the distinction may not always be easy, but once you see the benefits, you'll develop more faith in what's inside your own heart.

18 Play in the Dirt

"They are much to be pitied who have not been . . . given a taste for nature in early life."

—Jane Austen, *Mansfield Park* (1814)

Getting dirty is a child's job. In some ways, grass stains, dirty fingernails, and caked mud contribute as much toward living in the present moment as meditation or prayer. How many times were you told "Don't get dirty!" only to proceed outside and get as filthy as you possibly could? Sure, we might have met some stern eyes and gotten a scolding afterward, but boy was it worth it. Besides, back then most of us didn't have to worry about doing the laundry; that was someone else's job. The consequences just didn't resonate, so we weren't afraid. Playing in the dirt allowed us to rebel and have fun at the same time.

We didn't want to worry about staying clean. That wasn't the point. Rather, we wanted to forget about the rational order with which we coexisted in our homes. When the ball rolled through a muddy puddle, we didn't think about how the dirt on our hands would find its way to the kitchen walls. When we jumped into the pile of gooey leaves, we didn't think about how hard it would be for our mothers or fathers to remove the stains from our white shirts. If we threw our sneakers off and traipsed around in socks instead, we just liked the feeling of the grass on our shoeless feet. Besides, we had pairs and pairs of socks in our dresser drawers.

As we got older, though, the thrill of becoming a mess waned. Too much trouble. Not worth the effort. Too many other important things to do. Yet playing in the dirt can still be cathartic. Walking barefoot in the sand may be all you need to wipe everything off your mental slate so that you can concentrate on the here and now. If you're an avid gardener (or pretend to be long enough to get a few plants into the ground), then you know about the mesmerizing effects of a little dirt.

When we play in the dirt, we give ourselves permission to let go. When I was very young I wanted very much to be a witch. I knew that, to become an effective sorcerer, I'd have to be proficient at creating potions and other witchlike brews. Perhaps you cooked up similar dishes in your backyard. Mine usually consisted of twigs, dirt, leaves, acorns, and, of course, some water. My goal was not to stay clean but to invent the thickest, most disgusting concoction in the world. The thicker the brew, the more powerful the spell. Not until I went back in the house and washed my hands did I feel like a mortal again. For me the dirt was my passageway to a childhood utopia—a place where I had control, where I could manipulate and be the lead puppeteer.

Ironically, one of the nicest parts about getting dirty is the cleanup that inevitably occurs afterward. Think of the mess in your kitchen after whipping up a gourmet meal or the way you feel after spending an entire day outdoors cleaning up your yard. Now think of your sparkling counters after putting away the last dish or the invigorating shower that makes you feel human again. Like so many activities in life, playing in the dirt is part of a cycle—in this case, a cycle that brings on a cleansing, a sense of renewal, a chance to start again.

Maybe your idea of playing in the dirt goes no further than getting a mud-mask facial. That counts. Who knows? The next time you may even have your entire body wrapped in seaweed.

A Clean Sweep

Even the dirt inside the house can clear your mind and provide a respite from the neat and ordered rigors of daily life. I've only done this a couple of times, but the satisfaction I derive from cleaning the underbelly of a refrigerator is nothing short of bliss. It's a filthy job and often leads to unprecedented discoveries of dust and grime.

Besides enhancing the efficiency and appearance of the refrigerator, eliminating the dirt offers an equally important benefit. At least for me, the act of getting dirty represents a form of freedom, a reason to let go of worries and angst. In our day-to-day lives, a spot, a drip, even a little crumb somehow has the power to diminish and make something less perfect. Yet if the point is to get dirty in the first place, well, the flaws and ultimate mess are expected outcomes. Indeed, the dirt gives us something to show for all our hard work and all our hard fun.

19 Swap Lunch

"It is better not to say lend. There is no lending in that house. There is only giving."
—PEARL S. BUCK, *THE GOOD EARTH* (1931)

WHEN I WAS IN ELEMENTARY SCHOOL, I used to eye other kids' lunches with unabashed curiosity. I was a buyer, not a bringer, so I was fascinated by what emerged from my classmates' brown paper bags and sixties-vintage lunch boxes. One girl, allergic to flour, used to bring sandwiches made with blue bread. Watching this girl remove the contents from her bag was a lot like watching a magic trick every day at noon. *Abracadabra! Make me a blue sandwich.*

I don't recall anyone trading lunch back then, especially with the blue-bread girl. I don't think it was allowed, which is probably why I marvel so when my own daughter confesses to trading an unwanted apple for some yummy canned fruit, thick with syrup. I'm not happy she's traded something wholesome for a packaged snack, but I'm delighted that she's embraced the spirit of trading one thing for another.

Swapping lunch is probably one of the first experiences associated with sharing. You're at once a giver and a taker, and the transaction itself offers numerous lessons in taking care of those around us, including ourselves. Trading one thing for another demonstrates our abilities to give up something to make another happy. Sure, you feel you're getting something more valuable than what's being given away, but each party benefits from the visible, often unexpected joy that results when the goods change hands.

Occasionally, my daughter will report a missing item in a classmate's lunch sack. "I shared my sandwich, Mom," she'll say in response to my asking, "Did you eat your lunch today?" Or, in the morning when I'm wrapping up goodies, she'll ask for extras so she can hand a few out to friends. I love her sense of bounty and her unhesitant tendency to ask for more.

With kids, a trade's a trade; they're focused on the transaction, the deal. Those adult feelings of altruism and fulfillment take a while to kick in. But when they do, years later, swapping something palpable for what you can only feel in your heart is one of the sweetest, unwritten contracts two people can ever have.

A few years ago, my friend Danielle told me about a tradition she's faithfully carried on with other like-minded loyalists. Every so often Danielle gathers with some friends for a "pink elephant party." In her words, one finds something around the house that is too "heinous to keep" yet too valuable to throw away. I was glad for the tutorial, especially when I recently attended a business meeting with a pink elephant theme. The item I brought must have truly been heinous, because it got passed around like a hot potato; no one wanted it! What makes this kind of swap so hilarious is the twisted notion of giving a gift that you truly don't like. Usually, when I buy a gift, it's something I think the receiver will enjoy, but it's also an item that I'd happily accept as well.

In the bigger picture, though, these trades have something to teach. I call it "pink elephant philanthropy." Over the years, our tastes may change, we grow out of old clothes, we want to unclutter our environments. It's easy to throw something away, especially when it's picked up right down your hall or at the end of your driveway. Yet it's a whole lot more fulfilling to give something away that may help or bring happiness to someone else.

As you swap favors—taking in your neighbor's mail, watching a friend's child, or picking something up for a friend on your way home—remember not to keep score. Focus instead on the circle of giving. Reciprocity is open-ended, with a flexible schedule. You might give something away, but don't expect anything in return. It'll come back when you least expect it.

A cheerful giver does not count the cost of what he gives. His heart is set on pleasing and cheering him to whom the gift is given.

—JULIAN OF NORWICH, *REVELATIONS OF DIVINE LOVE* (1373)

20 Skip Class

"I can sometimes resist temptation, but never mischief."

—JOYCE REBETA-BURDITT, *THE CRACKER FACTORY* (1977)

ONE MORNING, as I watched the local news, the anchorman announced that it was International Goof Off Day. I'd never heard of this holiday. Still, I wondered how many people were planning to goof off. So I conducted a little test. I simply did my regular thing and waited for someone to come up to me and say, "Leslie, happy Goof Off Day!" Well, the painter showed up before seven A.M. and began to paint. My children went off to school with little protest. And things progressed as they normally do on a Wednesday. Not once did anyone wish me a happy Goof Off Day.

Still, I am a big proponent of taking entire days off—and half-days, too—to regroup, to achieve some kind of balance, and, very simply, to have fun. I could probably count on one hand the number of times I actually skipped class. Well, before I started college anyway. Not showing up in high school was always a fantasy, but guilt would course through my body every time I thought of taking off. These days, I still fantasize, but instead of letting those fantasies fade, I try to plan out a few and incorporate them into my patchwork life.

One of my favorite getaways is the one that starts in the newspaper. One day—when a deadline can wait or your presence isn't absolutely, positively necessary—check the movie listings, pick a show, buy yourself a ticket and some popcorn, and rest your weary bones inside the darkness of a theater. Later, instead of jumping up as the movie ends, stay for the credits, to squeeze out just a few more minutes of solitude. Of course, if you can persuade a friend to join you, by all means make your afternoon matinee a party.

One of my favorite outings occurred when my friend Linda and I visited the Art Institute of Chicago in the middle of the day, in the middle of the week. With our kids in school, we were golden until about three, when the school buses would begin rolling through the streets. First, we sat through a lecture by an actress who played the part of Georgia O'Keeffe. Next, we snaked through the gift shop scarfing up a few one-in-a-million deals. Then, with a little time to spare, we grabbed a light lunch at a Russian restaurant and returned home. Later that day, I couldn't help feeling as if I'd just gotten back from a short intercontinental excursion.

Initiating a "ditch day" should not be complicated. Indeed, perusing the classifieds for nearby yard and estate sales can be the beginning of an incredibly fun and fruitful adventure. Taking a spur-of-the-moment field trip is another exciting way to leave behind what will surely be waiting upon your return. You might even pretend to be a tourist in your own town and visit landmarks that you've never really noticed in your hurried past. Go to a baseball game and eat the worst junk food you can think of, including cotton candy. Get tickets to the circus and buy yourself a magic wand on your way out. Go to the library and browse aimlessly. Set aside a few hours and visit a day spa. Or decide, once and for all, that you're going to take that drive you've always dreamed of—

something that will take you far away from the normal, day-to-day grind that can rob you of the serendipitous fun that is synonymous with skipping class.

The Other R & R: Retreat & Refuge

A favorite possibility for escape is the journey toward a quiet retreat, a place that's a little familiar but clearly different from your everyday surroundings. Maybe it's somewhere that you've always wanted to visit but never had the time. Perhaps its pull is the solitude it offers, the chance to actually hear yourself think. It might be a place where your spirit can be restored, especially following a daunting life experience. Try to keep a mental list of destinations that will help you restore, rediscover, and reawaken what is buried deep within. A good friend might offer her home as a middle-of-the-day refuge. A secluded bench in a nearby park could be all you need. Find what's right for you.

21 Revel in the Next Best Thing

"Whatever is—is best."

ELLA WHEELER WILCOX, *POEMS OF PLEASURE* (1888)

SOME THINGS ARE WORTH WAITING FOR. The love of your life. The sequel to your favorite movie. A great shoe sale. These are just a few. Occasionally, however, we resign ourselves to the next best thing. In some cases, we can even look back and admit that we were better off taking seconds in the first place.

Some kids' eyes were always on the prize. Number two wasn't good enough. This drive to be the winner tended to come from external sources—a parent, a teacher, a coach. Yet many of us, especially those who couldn't run the fastest or jump the highest, derived our satisfaction and comfort from just knowing we had tried. Besides, the words "Try your best" were three of the most compassionate words we ever heard. Deep inside, we knew we couldn't be the first or the best at everything.

Many cultures rarely reward second bests or those who cross the finish line long after the spectators have gone home. Still, being number two or three or four is OK, especially if improvements are made along the way. When we don't reach the zenith, we also have an opportunity to demonstrate our resilience. Kids are especially good at picking themselves up after a fall. When I see this happen, I sometimes think about my own disappointments, wondering if I have the same zest to bounce back. With kids, the next opportunity to shine never seems far away. Just as their suns begin to set, they discover a second star over another horizon. Their quest for something good begins again.

We, too, can scout out other stars, secondary joys that, in the end, look nothing like the "lesser than" we might originally have imagined. To do this, however, we must give up our addiction to the "best" of everything: first place. First in line. First class. First prize. Everything else is second, not good enough, maybe even deficient. Not exactly self-esteem building. And while we learn early on that there will always be people who have more than we do and people who have less, this piece of wisdom doesn't necessarily make us feel any better.

That's when we have to look deep inside. Sometimes painful and occasionally time-consuming, looking inward may uncover undiscovered opportunities. Examining your spirit may also motivate you to relinquish the "gotta be the best" mantra that may very well have propelled you to the top but now feels like a huge burden. Remember, too, that the best is not necessarily the best for you. Think of the way a fragrance manifests itself differently on different people. What's enhancing for one person may be overwhelming for you.

Our desire to have the best and to be the best is closely related to our need to have more than we have. As children, we hear "no" whenever our desire for more is denied. As we grow older, however, the voice of denial becomes increasingly internal. "No, I don't need that," you might say to yourself, or "I'll wait until I can really afford" whatever it is you want.

If you're vying for the best or for more of something, settling for less may get you to where you need to be. Surprisingly, that may be enough. If *settling for something* bothers you, replace it with *accepting something*. Accepting something less than what you'd originally hoped for implies a certain graciousness, an understanding of what you do have. It's sort of a half-full, half-empty way of looking at things.

You won't always know what the next best thing may be. On first glance, it may not look so good. Still, all of us have the power to manipulate our environments and, at the very least, make an attempt to turn something sour into something sweet. Is it the silver lining in every disappointment? Maybe. But perhaps it's our ability to choose what we'll do if we can't be the first or we can't have the best. Indeed, we can choose to revel in whatever comes next.

22 Kiss a Frog

"Frog or pearl, life hid something at the bottom of the cup."
—MARY BUTTS, *ASHE OF RINGS* (1925)

I THINK THE PRINCESS in the famed Grimm fairy tale went through an awful lot to find her prince. She drops her ball, makes a promise she doesn't intend to keep, and then gets in trouble with her father, the king. All because she couldn't find immediate beauty in a kind and compassionate amphibian. OK, so she learned a lesson and they lived happily ever you-know-what. But do you really need to go to all that trouble to find a prince or, for that matter, to discover something beautiful? Beauty is so abundant, even if it's not within immediate reach, it's not hard to find. Indeed, it might be right in front of your nose, something you take for granted until someone else points it out.

What's always stayed with me about beauty are its contradictions. To some, beauty is strictly about looks. Yet how then do we explain our attraction to those who might not turn heads but exude charm, grace, and elegance through everything they do? Most of us are taught to value the beauty within. Yet we're still smitten by good looks, which is why frogs don't always get the chance they deserve. Obvious beauty, the kind that stares back at you from a movie screen or a fashion magazine, is hard to resist. It's like searching for a hotel room and then finally seeing a bright, blinking neon sign informing passersby of a vacancy.

Often, it's the subtle beauty that is more accessible and, in many cases, more real. An old, dilapidated house, for instance, might scream *condemned* and *unlivable*. An architect with an innate interest in design and a classically trained background might see the same structure and behold not only possibilities but beauty in its detail and historical significance.

Sometimes beauty, like a solid friendship, requires a long growing season. Think of an outdoor scene you've passed a million times. One day, though, maybe traffic has slowed you down, so you pause just long enough to look out the window. There in the distance you see it: a tree wearing the boldest autumnal red, and it takes your breath away. Or maybe you've gotten to know someone whose smile brings out the best in everyone. You never noticed it before, but then one day you make the connection. It's the smile, you say, almost out loud.

Beauty is not static. It changes form, especially when it is in the eye of the beholder. You may remember a beloved friend as looking one way. Yet when you're reunited, she may be different, maybe not as you remembered. Maybe older. Yet what you see is beautiful. What you see is timeless.

Nature, too, offers a timeless and inspiring kind of beauty. Depending upon where you live, seasons are marked by the appearance and disappearance of color. In the spring and summer, walking outside may feel as if you're walking straight into a vibrant painting. The multicolored leaves of fall make you breathless. Then winter arrives, and for many this marks the beginning of a long wait until the first robin appears or the quietest crocus peeks out of the softening ground. Yet winter is not without its beauty. On a sunless day, the grays merge to form a somber and peaceful landscape. Think of the silhouette of a leafless tree. Its leafy abundance may be missing, but its beauty is still intact.

For me, winter often serves up a wellspring of precious childhood memories packed with hours of sledding and big mugs of marshmallow- and whipped-cream-topped hot chocolate. What can you remember? How about a few magnificent snow days spent playing outdoors?

When you kiss a frog, it may eventually become a handsome prince or a beautiful house or a newly tailored dress or anything that at first seemed mediocre and plain. On the other hand, it may remain a frog. A plain, old greenish, web-footed frog. No surprises. No waiting for something better. Nonetheless, that frog could bring you more unexpected joy than you could possibly imagine, the kind of joy that sees nothing but beauty. After all, although a kiss is just a kiss, a frog may not always be just a frog.

Beauty Becomes the Beholder

Sometimes we see beauty through someone else's eyes. My friend Chris speaks fondly of someone she knows whose descriptions of beauty are poetic. While talking, her friend takes on a beauty that is as magnificent as the object he is describing. Similarly, reading about a place you've never been and may never get to visit can make you feel as if you have been there or, at the very least, prepare you for what you will see if you ever do go. When we listen to other voices, we get to know what we might never get to see. What a gift to treasure over and over.

Kiss a frog

23 Cry Over Spilled Milk

"Rich tears! What power lies in those falling drops."
—MARY DELARIVIERE MANLEY, *THE ROYAL MISCHIEF* (1696)

WHEN I WAS YOUNG I reacted to spilling my milk with Pavlovian consistency. Just like the dog that drooled as soon as it heard the bell, I would break into tears as soon as the glass tipped over. It always seemed so unbelievable that I could lose my grip on such a regular basis. I don't remember being scolded for creating the mess. Still, I followed up each spill with an eruption that successfully shifted everyone's attention from the tumbled glass and puddle of milk to a little girl's deafening wails.

Many of us grew up in an era when, after the initial outpour, tears were discouraged. Someone would quickly wipe them away, brush off our pants or skirts if we had fallen, and send us back from where we came.

Teachers, mothers and fathers, even the parents of our friends cajoled: "No need to cry over spilled milk." In other words, the damage has been done, there's nothing you can do about it, so forget it. Regardless of their well-intentioned instructions, some of us might have still felt bad, and a little extra crying might have helped us—in our own way, in our own time—forget and move on.

The problem with denying our tears—no matter why they fall—is that we negate and practically renounce a part of ourselves. Sadness, regret, grief, frustration, resentment: these are natural human emotions that beget tears. They are part of us. Society tells us where we can and can't cry. You can cry at funerals and weddings, but you can't cry at work or in front of your children. You can cry with your head sandwiched between two pillows in the middle of the night, but you can't cry in the grocery store.

One friend of mine broke down in the middle of a crowded store during a holiday shopping season. Overcome by what often occurs in the midst of holiday madness, she succumbed to the short fuses, rudeness, and general lack of kindness. "Everyone was grabbing things and speaking in such mean-spirited tones," she said. "I just couldn't take it and started to cry right there." Clearly, she was having a bad shopping day. But something else was bothering her as well. She wasn't looking forward to the holidays—her mother was ill and her parents were about to split up.

Sometimes tears are really a letting go of a storm of emotions, emotions that can't distinguish between a public place like a store and a more private spot like your bathtub or kitchen table. Crying is cathartic. When we cry, we extract, piece by piece, our stress and allow the healing process to begin. This can happen anywhere.

Crying also cleanses. One of my favorite places to weep is the shower. If you want to cry and get clean at the same time, the sound of the water and its heat and power may be the perfect backdrop to your tears. Not only will the water rinse away your tears, it will sweep them down the drain, an obvious metaphor that can help you regroup and prepare yourself for whatever comes next.

Children cry because they are hurt and want attention (or a piece of candy or a toy). We, too, cry when we are hurt and want to be noticed. Yet the kind of attention we seek is different. Crying loses its manipulative powers as we get older. But that doesn't minimize our need to sob every once in a while. Crying over spilled milk or shattered crystal or burned cookies or anything that you deem catastrophic is OK. Crying soothes and comforts. It allows us to be tender and kind to ourselves and, hence, to others. Tears turn us inside out so that both our joy and sorrow can coexist. After all, one is very often followed by the other. Besides, I know for a fact that big girls do cry.

24 Happy Birthday to You

"It is lovely, when I forget all birthdays, including my own, to find that somebody remembers me."

—ELLEN GLASGOW, *LETTERS OF ELLEN GLASGOW* (1958)

WHEN IS YOUR BIRTHDAY? Will you take the day off and celebrate? It only comes around once a year, and although you may not be planning a big bash, it's still a good reason to rejoice.

Celebrating the day you were born is the perfect way to start again. Though you may think back to past celebrations and wonder where all the time has gone, this year's birthday is what counts the most. And although the Western New Year begins on January first, your birthday is the start of something as well. Indeed, your birthday really is the first day of the rest of your life. It's also the one day of the year that's all about you.

For a child, a birthday is possibly the best day of the year. I know some kids who begin planning their birthday fetes a full year before the date. Who will I invite? Where will it be? What will I get? The questions swirl around for months, and before we know it, we're planning the next one. On our birthdays, we were queens and kings for a day. Maybe you had breakfast in bed or you got to pick your all-time favorite dish for dinner. Every breath felt exhilarating on that day. We wore permanent smiles. We felt special.

As an adult, I try to celebrate my birthdays with some self-indulgence, but I also think long and hard about the bigger picture—what I've learned all these years and what might be in store after I've blown out the candles and eaten a slice of cake (with a scoop of ice cream).

Yet it's easy to let our own birthdays slide. A deadline looms. A spouse is out of town. It's a weeknight and there's just too much to do. You may not have even told anyone. But neglecting your special day means giving up the chance to recognize your presence in the world. Perhaps if we all jotted down our birthdays on the calendars we buy once a year, remembering and celebrating wouldn't be so hard to do.

I know a woman who makes it easy for others to celebrate her birthday. Whenever she visits a friend's home, she scouts out a calendar and quietly records the date of her birth. It may be a wall calendar hanging on the back of a kitchen door or even a fancy datebook that rests on a friend's desk. The nice part, she says, is that friends always call her on her birthday.

Several years ago, I had a boss who celebrated birthdays by asking his employees, "What have you learned?" It's the only time I can remember having been asked that question on my birthday. When I turned forty, many people asked nervously, "So, how does it feel?" To be old? To have said good-bye to my thirties? That was a hard question to answer. But "What have you learned?" gave me pause and forced me to think. I don't recall what I said then, but on every birthday since I've asked myself the same question.

For many, a birthday means opening presents and, later, writing notes of thanks and appreciation. Yet it's also a time to reflect on the intangible gifts we've received over the year and to be grateful for what others have done on our behalf. We may have come into this world alone, but if we're lucky, we've had a lot of company along the way. Birthdays are a good time to acknowledge the gifts we've taken from others.

Our birthdays are also occasions for self-study, self-awareness. This can be an extraordinary gift, especially if your life is brimming over with too much to do. Have you ever been so busy that, for a small moment, you could no longer recognize yourself? Even on the busiest day, our birthdays remind us of who we are and where we've come from.

My father-in-law once shared some wisdom that is particularly relevant to birthdays. Every morning he looks into the mirror. "If I see myself," he says, "I'm a winner." On your next birthday, look into the mirror. If you see yourself, consider yourself a winner. Then go one step further: take a closer look. You might see something new, something you haven't noticed in the past. And don't forget to wish yourself a happy, happy birthday.

The Story of Your Life

If your birthday is approaching, consider telling friends the story of your life. My friend Chris once attended a birthday gathering where the honoree simply shared the highlights of her fifty years. For about an hour she had the floor. Her friends got to hear a story, and she got to celebrate and honor a great milestone. What a simple though meaningful way to say "Happy Birthday."

25 "What's Your Favorite Color?"

"Variety is the soul of pleasure."

—Aphra Behn, *The Rover*, part 2 (1681)

"I only have *sixteen*, Mom," said my daughter, referring to the paltry amount of crayons stored away in her desk at school. I had just pulled out of a bag Crayola's vintage 64-count box of crayons. "Look what I bought for your brother!" I exclaimed, truly thinking she'd share my enthusiasm. What we ended up sharing, however, is our collective love for as many crayons as we can get our hands on.

"Look!" she exclaimed. "There's even a sharpener in the back." That did me in. I was back in Mrs. DeWitt's first-grade class, sitting quietly, deciding—in my little girl, demure fashion—which color I would use next. Remembering this, as my son approached us, luck and the magic of distraction enabled me to successfully lift the box out of sight and quickly into my daughter's backpack for a one-way trip to fourth grade.

Not unlike the little girl I recalled, staring at the box of crayons, my daughter wants to experience the full range of color. She doesn't worry much about adhering to some arbitrary set of rules governing the placement of one color next to another. As a result, her imagination is still intact. Fortunately, the anxiety that we encounter as adults hasn't hit her yet.

If color has faded out of your vista, consider drawing it back in. Color can dramatically change our lives. Look at the seasons. How many colors make up the fall and spring? What about the expression on a hospital patient's face when flowers are delivered?

I have an unopened box of crayons in my office—the sixteen-count variety. Unlike my daughter, though, I'm happy with these perfectly pigmented sticks of wax. I've never opened the box, but I know they're in there just waiting to be used. It also reminds me that it's best to leave the black-and-white world behind and, instead, try to add color to my days. A black-and-white world— one where things are either this or that, with no in-between— restricts our movements and perceptions. Color teaches us to be open-minded. A black-and-white frame of mind presumes that anything gray is neither valid nor true. An outlook that encompasses color magnifies the possibilities and helps us to see beyond ourselves.

My favorite artwork is exhibited close to home. In my kitchen, actually, where my kids' drawings and paintings hang on two pantry doors. Commentary by our visitors is always positive and usually evokes a question or two that my children are happy to answer. Even the people who don't actually say anything about the pictures communicate through their expressions their appreciation for our display of bold colors.

As children, we were encouraged to experiment with color. Mix green and blue. What do you get? How about red and yellow? Color suggests variety. And variety helps us remove the shackles of conformity and the average of anything. In some ways, we've become a culture of neutralizing. The real estate agent counsels the home seller to paint the walls off-white. A neighborhood association frowns on someone's newly painted pink front door. And black is the well-known wardrobe staple—the little black dress, the three dozen pairs of black shoes, and the quintessential don't-go-anywhere-without-it black jacket.

In the last few years, however, I've noticed a few promising trends. Cellular phones, for instance, are now available in a cornucopia of colors. A few years ago nail polish exploded into yellows, blues, greens, and other brilliant hues. Even our computers are beginning to look like Popsicles.

It's not necessary to completely wash yourself in a rainbow. Accents are adequate and, for many cases, preferable. Color breathes life and shape into what otherwise might appear flat and barren. Color reflects our universe and hence your life. Think back to an early science class. Color helps us differentiate between two otherwise identical objects. Color makes our lives vivid. It invigorates, characterizes, and wakes up our souls. It is also the essential ingredient for painting your most prized possession: your life's canvas, your masterpiece.

Hue Are You?

Here are some ways to add color to your life:

- Paint a room with a color you've always liked.
- Fill your garden with a variety of flowers.
- Next time you go to a party, don't wear black.
- Pour rainbow sprinkles on your cereal (or ice cream).
- For one day, use a purple pen instead of the classic blue or black.
- Dress your bed in a set of colorful sheets.
- Bring your lunch to work in a brightly-colored reusable bag.
- Buy yourself a bouquet of flowers at least once a month.
- Fill a salad with lots of different colored vegetables.
- Visit an art gallery and, on your way out, buy a colorful postcard reproduction.

26 Don't Be Afraid of the Mean Girl

"Nothing in life is to be feared. It is only to be understood."
— MARIE CURIE, IN DONALD O. BOLANDER ET AL., *INSTANT QUOTATION DICTIONARY*
(1969)

WE'VE ALL MET THE MEAN GIRL. She poked fun at your new haircut or told the whole class that your dress was out of style. She's the one who inspired fear and even a twisted, albeit fleeting, respect among your friends. Who was this girl, anyway? And why, for goodness' sake, did she pick on you?

Chances are, you had little to do with her peccadilloes. Something else was probably eating away at the good parts inside of her. And we all know that mean girls generally don't feel happy unless someone else is feeling bad. Should we even consider them human?

As children, we develop a special radar for people like this (boys can be mean, too). As adults, we hone the skill and use it to carefully pick and choose our friends and acquaintances. Sometimes the mean girl isn't exactly mean; she may be the controlling type who, every once in a while, says mean things, things that leave you wondering, now why would she have said that? The mean girl can be subtle. She may not exactly be mean to you but is mean-spirited with a negative disposition. And although she will never come right out and criticize, she will let you know in every possible way that she doesn't approve and that you don't measure up.

As children, many of us were taught to be nice to the mean girl. "Kill 'em with kindness," our mothers and grandmothers used to say. If we were nice to the mean girls, they'd leave us alone, right?

Not always. Because no matter how adept we became at ducking out of the mean girl's reach, like the unsuspecting fly, we occasionally got caught in her web. Even today, I think the mean girl sometimes finds her way into our lives. I'm not talking about the shop clerk who snarls when you pull out your checkbook in the cash-only line. I'm referring to someone whose presence is not so fleeting, someone who's in your life whether you like it or not.

The mean girl doesn't necessarily inspire fear. Nor will you always detect a smirk on her face. She might simply be an annoyance, the uneven square of sidewalk that, if you're not careful, will bring you to your knees every time. In some cases, you'll be unable to pinpoint the source of your discomfort. She simply gets under your skin. Well-meaning friends may suggest that you confront her, though your instincts may tell you just to walk away.

You've heard the story about the man who keeps walking down the same street and falls into the same hole each time. Well, finally, he begins to walk around the hole and then eventually decides, wisely, to walk down a different street altogether. During the course of my life I've taken a similar path, after first taking a bit of a beating. But then, one day, I woke up a little more alert, a little smarter. I realized, finally, that there was another way to go, another way to be.

One way to step off the old path and onto the new—*and* to avoid falling into a hole—is to prepare yourself for the consequences. So many of us want to be liked, and, as a result, we do or say things that aren't always consistent with our true selves. When you're true to yourself—essential if you want to be free of the mean girl—someone may not like you. And that's OK. The funny thing is this: as we step out of the mean girl's path, we may feel a little unkind, as if our avoidance is a display of bad manners. And although I agree with writer Amelia E. Barr, who wrote in 1913 that kindness is always fashionable, I think the purest form of kindness is the compassion we bestow upon ourselves, truly the epitome of high style.

The Mean Girl Within

Few of us claim to be angels 100 percent of the time. There are moments, though, when we begin to resemble the mean girl we so dislike, and we rarely recognize when we are headed breezily down a mean-girl path. If you ever begin to feel like the mean girl, don't be afraid of her in yourself either. She's probably trying to tell you something that isn't obvious and may possibly be painful. So listen carefully, look deep inside, and then wait a little while. You may hear a voice that you have previously chosen to ignore. But listen anyway. It may speak a truth that you need to hear.

27 Talk to Yourself

"You can live a lifetime and, at the end of it, know more about other people than you know about yourself."

—BERYL MARKHAM, *WEST WITH THE NIGHT* (1942)

DID YOU EVER TALK TO YOURSELF when you were a kid? When you were sure a snake had slithered under your sheets or the bogeyman was standing inside your closet? We talked to ourselves when the lights went out in a storm or when some bully was approaching on the playground. As a young girl, I talked to myself all the time. This chatter paved the way for a glorious trip into my imagination. Sometimes I was a witch casting my favorite spells. Other times, in a small upstairs study, I tried, by hiding out and writing in a diary, to relate to Anne Frank. In some circles, the virtues of talking to yourself go unnoticed or, worse, it is discouraged. Yet when we engage in self-chatter, we get to know ourselves a little better. And each time we gather more data, like a navy captain immersed in a submarine beneath the sea, we become better navigators. When we hear ourselves speak, it can help us become more whole, more of who we really are.

Sometimes, when I'm particularly bored or resentful of what I'm doing, I'll mutter something like, "I hate doing this!" Maybe I'm plunging the toilet or cleaning the oven. For one friend, talking to herself means she stays on track. "Okay, first I have to do this. Next, I have to do that," she'll tell herself as she moves through her busy days. Maybe you occasionally say something out of sheer embarrassment. You drop all your packages on the way to the car and say to no one in particular, "How did that happen?"

Often, we talk to ourselves as we try to find some resolution. This is especially true when we're faced with a choice that could have a major impact on our lives. So we speak with two points of view, hoping that we can arrive at the right answer. Even if you don't hear an answer—or the response you were hoping for—you've still allowed yourself to vent, to calmly release what had been boiling inside. We might even engage in these conversations following a vexing occurrence. "I can't believe what just happened here," you mutter to yourself quietly, in a way validating the experience.

Talking to yourself can be like entering the safest place on Earth. Indeed, the dialogue between you and . . . you is great preparation for the really big moments. Judy, a nurse I know, shared a wonderful story about the time she passed her board exams. As she left for work one day, she clutched an envelope that had just arrived. It contained the results of what must have been hours of study. As she walked out of her apartment building in downtown Chicago, she stopped, still grasping the envelope. "Should I open it or not?" She questioned *talk to yourself* herself over and over until she finally attracted the attention of an elderly woman passing by.

"Are you OK?" the woman asked. Judy told the stranger that she was holding the most important letter of her life. "Well, are you going to *open* it?" said the woman, who clearly had walked by at a moment when Judy needed her most. Judy opened the envelope, shared her good news, and received a congratulatory hug from someone she hasn't seen since.

Not surprisingly, self-talk has a lot to do with self-validation, a constant struggle for me. A friend once said that sometimes she'll talk to herself with a very specific message. When things don't go well for her with a friend, she'll remind herself, quite audibly, that she still has herself. Sometimes just the sound of our own voices is enough—at least for the moment—to steady the shaky ground beneath us. If you listen hard, you might hear what you probably already know: other people don't—and can't—make us unimportant. We're important, meaningful individuals because of what we say, what we think, what we do. Amazing, isn't it, how a few unscripted lines brought out from below the surface can make us feel a little better about ourselves? It's like a pantomime for our hearts—that vital organ that may not have a speaking part on the grand stage of life but appears in every scene, just the same.

Sticks and Stones and Words, Too

As we grow up, we realize that just like those sticks and stones, words really can hurt. We can't control what other people say, but we can use our own words carefully, especially when we're talking to ourselves. Sometimes, I'll hear a voice that is terribly self-critical, even cruel. It says things to me that I wouldn't say to a best friend. I keep listening though, because eventually I realize something truly stunning and wonderful. The words don't reflect me; rather, they're expressions that I've incorporated into my self-speak. At this point, I toss the words out of my personal glossary, much like I would throw out a piece of bad fruit. If this happens to you, try to catch yourself and put those words where they belong—with the sticks and stones, as far away as possible.

28 Don't Get Rattled by "The Look"

"No more pencils, no more books. No more teacher's dirty looks."
—TRADITIONAL CHILDREN'S NURSERY RHYME

YOU'VE SEEN *THE LOOK*. That over-the-top nonverbal form of expression. It silently admonishes, puts a child firmly in her or his place, and stops the most verbose from opening their mouths. Maybe you've been the object of such looks, or perhaps you're a master at delivering this inaudible form of communication. Consider the following, which might even be registered in some obscure section of the U.S. Patent and Trademark office: "Don't even think of touching that!" or "I can't believe what you just said!" or this popular glance: "Don't even go there."

The troubling part of this voiceless vernacular isn't necessarily the look itself but rather our childlike reaction to it. In the past, especially as a child, I was rattled by the look. Even now, I am startled by its power. Sometimes a sideways glance from my daughter is enough to shorten my five-foot, six-inch frame. The irony, of course, is that in some cases I will return the favor with one of my own wide-eyed faces that hopefully says, "Yes? Do you have something to say to me?" For me, though, that's the triumph. Communicating with our features may be all we have in some circumstances. Yet when we use *the look* to belittle others, instead of using words to educate or inform them, we're not being kind—to them or ourselves.

Most positive nonverbal cues—warm and welcoming touches, smiles, a sympathetic nod—are like the colorful and sweet sprinkles we toss on cupcakes and ice cream (for breakfast, of course). They enhance human interaction.

But the glaring and rolling eyes are another story. Have you returned merchandise that still had the receipt attached? You walk into the store, clutching the receipt. You may have even made a copy that's safely folded inside your wallet. You've anticipated a disdainful look from the store clerk, and, sure enough, you are right. You're given no sympathy, and when it's all over and you're walking out of the store, you're convinced that you are the first person in history to have ever had the nerve to ask for a refund or contritely accepted credit.

Unfortunately, we tend to overreact to external forces like looks and criticism when something is eating away at us inside. Forget about the damage that may occur with sticks and stones. A look can positively annihilate. Yet even if we haven't uncovered the source of our vulnerabilities on any given day, I believe that it's possible to avoid the psychic skirmish that a look can set into motion. The trick is to leave those external forces exactly where they came from—on the outside.

You can't control them anyway. Even those menacing looks, the "looks that can kill," are, in reality, harmless. Think of them as the billboards you pass at sixty miles an hour: "Oh, that's nice; I'll give it some thought." On some days it takes tremendous fortitude to respond with no response at all. We heard the advice as kids—"Just ignore it!"—and as adults we dole it out, forgetting sometimes what a difficult task that can be.

But think about it: how much more energy does it take to react to a look versus keeping that look at bay and disallowing it from entering your frame of mind? It may not feel exactly meditative, but letting it pass will help you get on to things that are much more important.

Part of recapturing the joys of childhood and finding them a home in your adult life is recognizing what may best be left behind. Feelings of powerlessness, for example, are not likely to bring more fun into your life. If you still get rattled by the look, consider sift-

ing through your past to pinpoint exactly where all these bad feelings come from. Once you've identified the starting point, cut off its lifeline to prevent it from intruding upon your present day. And try this: the next time someone tries to rattle you with the look, mentally draw a mustache above the lips. If you have time, scribble in a couple of horns and a tail, too.

29 Talk to Strangers

"Strangers . . . are just your friends that you don't know yet."
—MARGARET LEE RUNBECK, *OUR MISS BOO* (1942)

A FEW DAYS AGO, as I sat in one of my favorite places to write, I talked to a stranger. I'd finished my coffee but lingered, hoping for more inspiration. This time, however, I would be inspired not by my own thoughts, but the friendly manner in which this woman reached out.

I'd taken a break between chapters and couldn't help noticing the crowded table next to me. The group was just breaking up when a woman stopped by to say hello. I was delighted but surprised as well. When I'm out writing, people frequently look down at my work but rarely comment. After all, most of us grew up with this steady parental refrain: *Don't talk to strangers.*

The warning, though well-intentioned, has a restrictive nature. It's one thing to mind your own business or stay out of someone's way when you sense danger. But where do you draw the line between acting safe and cutting yourself off from the world? It's true that most of us don't connect with everyone we meet. And some people are more naturally introverted and prefer to keep strangers at a comfortable distance.

But for every stranger we ignore, we forfeit the chance to bring more joy into our lives. I'm not suggesting that you strike up a conversation with each person you see. But when we talk to strangers and open ourselves up to someone new and different, we also uncover a galaxy of opportunities—opportunities to graciously accept the generosity of someone previously unknown, to discover something in common with a person who may over time become a dear friend, to step onto a path of self-discovery, and to finally have faith in the kindness of strangers. Allow a stranger to drop into your life and you may learn something new and gain a different perspective. After confessing to a fellow traveler that I didn't like to fly, he offered immediate comfort. "I just don't get how the plane stays in the air," I whispered. "Speed," said the engineer sitting next to me. I'll never forget him or his lucid description of how planes fly. Just listening made me feel better.

In most cases, we never see these people again, and there's no risk: there's freedom in telling a stranger something we'd normally not share with a person we know. Yet the strangers we meet just once are often as memorable as the people we see every day. Think of the disgruntled crowd waiting out a storm on the runway or huddled inside by the gate, where it's standing room only. Crises and moments of inconvenience frequently bring strangers together. It makes the waiting not so long, the loneliness not so deep, the passage of time a little more enjoyable.

One of the most provocative books I've ever read focuses on this very issue. In *The Kindness of Strangers: Penniless Across America*, author Mike McIntyre shares a journey that took him, cashless, through the heart and soul of the United States. He relied on the kindness of people he'd never met before. What I learned from *The Kindness of Strangers* has a lot to do with my faith in the unknown. With enough faith, that place called the unknown, and perhaps the strangers who inhabit that place, becomes not a murky and unfamiliar destination but rather a serendipitous and comfortable spot somewhere in your future. And in that strand of time not yet lived, the perfect in "perfect stranger" takes on a benevolence that could change your life forever.

Talk Is Cheap

It's easy to incorporate a little friendliness into your day. Here are a few tricks to keep up your sleeve:

- Promise yourself to smile and say hello to three strangers per day.
- Say "thanks" to the trash collector.
- Instead of hanging up on a telemarketer, just say, "I'm not interested, but thanks for calling."
- Introduce yourself to a neighbor you've never met.
- If you ride a bus, tell the driver to have a good day as you're stepping off.

30 Eat the Dough

"This body of ours has one fault: the more you indulge it, the more things it discovers to be essential to it. It is extraordinary how it likes being indulged."
—St. Teresa of Avila, *The Way of Perfection* (1579)

SOMETIMES YOU'VE JUST GOT TO EAT THE WRONG FOODS. Brownie batter. Chocolate-chip cookie dough. Three bowls of Jell-O. Nothing but small pleasures and 100 percent indulgence.

Growing up, small pleasures meant the presentation of a beater or two covered with the drippings of what later would become a plate of cookies. Somehow that delicious preview made the waiting a little easier, a little less maddening. If we were lucky, we got the bowl, too, the childlike equivalent to winning the lottery. Later, whatever emerged from the oven felt like a second helping, a bonus. Perhaps you sampled my own idea of the perfect cookie: a bazillion chocolate chips stuck into a ball of uncooked dough. Licking the spoon—even asking for a little dough—seemed like a positively natural and essential part of baking.

A slight indulgence of what is purportedly bad for you can be mighty powerful. It's an easy and surefire way to know that the sky won't fall simply because you've sampled a piece of heaven. Indeed, sometimes an ounce of pleasure is all we need to march bravely forward, at least until we go to bed at night.

I know someone who confessed to having a single piece of chocolate a day. I always thought that was such a perfect expression of enjoying, on a regular basis, a minor indulgence. Yet more than her actual consumption of what I'm sure wasn't just *any* piece of chocolate was her decision to treat herself—on a daily basis—to something she loves. It cleverly demonstrated both self-love and restraint.

Indulging in life's small pleasures isn't just for planned, special occasions. Sampling a sinful slice of something should feel the same as finding a $10 bill on the street. It's an unexpected, nice surprise that may not happen on a daily basis but, in a whimsical and wonderful way, makes one day truly stand out. Embrace a whimsical moment as if you're accepting a dare, testing yourself beyond your normal limit. As kids, we dared everyone but ourselves to do the outlandish, to shock and amaze. "I dare you to knock on Mrs. So-and-So's door." "I dare you to pull your shirt up!" "I dare you to eat the whole thing!" Eating the dough lets you bring back the dare, only this time you're the one living dangerously, the one who gets a chance to taste the triumph.

So, once in a while, reconnect with one of childhood's most innocuous forms of good living. Even a finger full of something gooey is probably enough to inspire a moment's worth of pure pleasure. Try it and look around. OK, so maybe the earth will move an inch or two. But I'll bet your complexion stays intact and your jeans still fit.

Living in Sin

It's not always easy to indulge in and treat ourselves to what's sublime. Too much fat, too much sugar, too much, too much, too much. Still, the pleasure derived from an infrequent delight can last long after you've swept up the last brownie crumb or spooned out the remaining melted ice cream. Give yourself a break every now and then by indulging with a crowd. Serve your favorite brand of brownies (or, if you're feeling especially industrious, make them from scratch), and serve them to a group of friends with the finest vanilla ice cream available, perhaps a batch of homemade. And don't forget to lick the spoon.

31 Make Up the Rules as You Go

"General rules are dangerous of application in particular instances."
—CHARLOTTE M. YONGE, *THE PILLARS OF THE HOUSE*, VOLUME 2 (1889)

SOMETIMES THE EASIEST RULES TO FOLLOW are the ones we make up as we go. We may draw on our own experiences. Occasionally, though, we benefit from the wisdom of others.

Last fall I heard writer Anne Lamott speak at a conference. At one point she compared the writing process to playing a game of Pick-Up Sticks. Looking out at the audience, she offered this simple though—for me—profound piece of advice. "Pick up the easy sticks first," she said.

So, a few months later, when I spotted a tall can of Pick-Up Sticks at a toy store, I thought of it as a talisman, a muse that could help me write the easy parts first, my new rule for writing. I quickly tossed the can into the cart and brought it home along with the toys I'd picked up for my kids. Usually the can stands next to my computer. Along with encouraging words from friends and family, this game has become my inspiration.

Not surprisingly, the can occasionally finds its way into my kids' rooms, where I serve as a compliant opponent. I never win this game. I lose when my daughter follows the rules. I lose when my son makes up the rules. But the look of enchantment on his face as he picks up one stick after the other—some touching, some not—makes my loss a sweet victory.

As he smiles his winning Mom-you're-not-going-to-stop-me smile, he deftly releases the sticks, which fan out into a peacock-

like arc upon the floor. Quickly, he plucks up
the easy sticks first. Eventually, though, he
brushes one stick against another or inadver-
tently leans his hand down and moves the
whole bunch. My competitive spirit awakens
and I reach down to take my turn.

"No!" he says, as he sweeps my hand out of
his way and proceeds to clear the floor. I try to
explain the rules, but he is intent on removing
each stick, one by one, without interruption. Maybe
he takes the game's name literally, I reason; he's just doing his thing
by picking up those sticks. But as we repeat the whole process, I
realize that he's just making up the rules as he goes. For the
moment, it suits him.

Call it improvisation or creativity. When we make up the rules
as we go, it feels like a smooth ride down a perfectly white, snowy
hill. Everything seems to fall into place, no one has gotten in your
way, you might even do it again tomorrow. Other days, though,
your unrehearsed movements may feel awkward, as if you are flying by the seat of your pants. But, eventually, even that shaky
ground seems to stabilize, making way for the confidence you need
to do it over again. All because you decided not to follow the rules.

Yet few of us can unscroll a set of rules for every situation.
We have to think on our feet. We have to make it up as we go. If
we don't make it up, we might end up in the same place, again and
again. And as comforting and familiar as that may feel, it's possible that what we're avoiding—an unknown abyss—is really
more of a great, unencumbered space. A space where energy fuels

creativity instead of anxiety. A space where going with the flow is driving down an expansive highway instead of a narrow path.

Without rules, we may feel more vulnerable, as if the looseness and lack of structure will lead us toward defeat. But rules can also be constricting, keeping us from stretching or even soaring every once in a while. If we can improvise—make up the rules as we go—it becomes easier to reach a middle ground, a place where rules help us grow and thrive.

Clearly, we can't always make up the rules as we go along. Indeed, some rules should be set in stone. For instance, cookies should not be eaten over a keyboard, and, in most cases, you should ask before taking something that belongs to someone else. Living by the rules, however—especially the ones we've reluctantly adopted as our own—can suffocate our ability to adapt to and embrace the unplanned moments of our daily lives.

Some rules force us to do things the hard way. So instead of picking up the easy sticks first, we construct unnecessary barriers that might prevent us from achieving success. Instead of going with the flow, we not only swim upstream, we wear ourselves down with a set of circumstances that have no relevance in our lives.

In the Taoist tradition, going with the flow is called *Wu Wei*. It means to act without acting. I love this phrase, especially its phonetic translation, which, to me, sounds like "woooooh weeeeee!" Wu Wei suggests that if we pay too much attention to obstacles, we lose sight of our options and see no way out.

When my son plays Pick-Up Sticks I think he is practicing a form of Wu Wei so he won't get stuck. I could protest his method. But that might drive him away. So I'm glad he makes up the rules as he goes and that he keeps picking up the easy sticks one by one.

32 "Guess What!"

"I felt it shelter to speak to you."

—EMILY DICKINSON, IN MABEL LOOMIS TODD, ED., *LETTERS OF EMILY DICKINSON*, VOLUME 2 (1894)

DO YOU REMEMBER SHARING SECRETS? We told secrets because otherwise we'd burst. Sometimes our secrets were nothing more than the funniest things we'd heard all day. We also whispered our most private thoughts. It helped us connect and establish closeness. It freed us, too, from keeping too much bottled up inside.

We all have secrets. We keep some for ourselves. Some we keep for others. The most precious secrets are the ones we share with trusted friends and family. When we confide in someone we trust, we expose a piece of ourselves without having to take cover. And as we let that piece float out into the open, we, in turn, let that person in. Compassion cancels out judgment. And for a split second, it feels like someone really is standing in our shoes.

We learn early on that secrets hold tremendous power. Indeed, on the playground secrets are the valuable currency of popularity and dominance. Hopefully, though, as we grow older, sharing our secrets becomes less about control and more about comfort.

Several years ago, after my husband and I decided to relocate from Washington, D.C., to Rochester, New York, I shared my news with a coworker who had grown up in a Rochester suburb. I walked into her office, shut the door behind me, and revealed my new secret. Patti's eyes grew wide and a smile emerged that I would have never imagined. "I love Rochester!" she exclaimed as the papers she'd been holding in her hand flew up into the air. "We used to shovel the driveway and then go inside and have pancakes for dinner."

My private news had found just the right home. Intellectually, I knew the move would be problematic, as most big changes like that are, but with the snow and pancakes image firmly ironed into my mind, I sensed that maybe everything would be all right. Patti kept my secret, reminding me of her understanding every so often with a knowing wink.

Sometimes our secrets turn into confessions. A new friend may have had a similar experience, and when you compare notes, you're both amazed by what you suddenly have in common. All at once, feelings of vulnerability and apprehension are replaced by the oneness that comes with a new bond.

When someone close to you shares something from deep within, it's as if the two of you are standing in the same shadow. It's that close. Yet occasionally we are told things we don't want to know. It feels as though someone dropped an old piano on our front step, with a note that says, "This is for you." But we have nowhere to put it. In these situations, you need to be able to give it back with a simple message that says, "I have no place to keep this."

If we're very lucky in life, our "guess whats!" are heard by the people who mean the most to us. And we're just as lucky if those same people look to us as a source of trust and confidence. When you set a secret free into the careful hands of someone you trust—someone who takes all of you—it's like two hearts beating together, in sympathy and in joy. And that's a wonderful thing.

33 "Are We There Yet?"

"The journey is my home."

—MURIEL RUKEYSER, "JOURNEY," *ONE LIFE* (1957)

HAVE YOU EVER ARRIVED SOMEWHERE only to discover that the journey mattered more than the destination? That the path itself had more to offer than the place where you could hang your hat? Sometimes we forget the richness of the journey, the serendipitous souvenirs that we can pick up along the way. Stopping to see how far we've gone and how much farther we have to go helps us enter more fully the flow of life and enjoy the movement that takes us from here to there.

As children, how many of us sang, almost in unison, "Are we there yet?" or my father's favorite, "When are we going to be there?"? Forget about our undeveloped sense of time, we simply had no patience. Anticipating our arrival made it nearly impossible to wait. Intent upon getting there, we didn't really pay attention to what we saw in between our driveways and our final destinations.

Yet the moments we collect from points *A* to *B* can be as purposeful as what we discover when we finally do arrive. Our points of departure are rich with possibilities—known and imagined. When we move from here to there—and back again—our perspectives change, our points of view expand. We might even abandon our fear of the unknown. Some of the best and most fruitful journeys are the ones that lead us inward toward a deeper understanding of where we fit in. A journey away from home gives us a chance to put into storage long-held beliefs that have the power to distort our interpretation of new places, new experiences. Indeed, traveling light applies not only to our clothes and other possessions but to our preconceived notions—judgments in waiting—that could otherwise wear us down.

You can lighten your load by breaking up the journey. Unexpected stops and detours may add miles to your trip, but those periodic pauses are not interruptions. In fact, they may turn out to be what everyone remembers best. Our pediatrician, Judith, confirmed this notion recently when she described her kids' unexpected delight in the ordinary offerings of a roadside rest stop. "Sometimes they have more fun on the way than with what awaits them on the other side," she says. Think of the child who expresses more glee for the hotel pool than the theme park down the road. Talk about finding the good things in your own backyard!

For many, a journey resembles anything but a straight line. Getting lost, stopping at a roadside fruit stand, going the long way around: these are the journeys that stop us from rushing through life, from getting somewhere as fast as we possibly can. Arriving on time at a business meeting or picking up your kid at day care before the doors close—these are noble pursuits. Giving in to a detour may add some miles to your distance. Yet the clarity you can achieve by slowing down—watching the ride—will, in many cases, make up for any lost time.

Often, what becomes clear has less to do with what we are expecting to find and more to do with where we've come from and how we've changed as a result of our journey. For me, a journey forever ties its destination to my home. Before I leave, I am at home, anticipating. When I arrive, I can't help but think about my home—who and what I miss, what I may bring back as a reminder of where I've been.

Not long ago, as I sat on a bench downtown, the woman next to me had this to say about her journey. "I took the bus in today," she said. "It beats the traffic, and I get to see the city neighborhoods." I admired her use of public transportation but was more intrigued by the sights she took in along the way. Later in the day as my son and I chugged along in the rush hour, I thought of the woman I'd talked to a few hours earlier. Clearly, I had not beat the traffic, but it was the slow movement of the cars and trucks that enabled us to look more closely at the buildings and billboards that ushered us in and out of our day downtown. Whenever we came to a complete standstill, we got to soak in a few city details—a small park and the juxtaposition of short residential buildings against the dramatic backdrop of 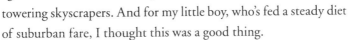 towering skyscrapers. And for my little boy, who's fed a steady diet of suburban fare, I thought this was a good thing.

For many, a journey is a search for home. We all want a place in the world, a place to call home. Even when we find it, that place isn't always easy to keep. Some of us find our place more quickly than others. We know it when we see it. Others, however, might revel in the quest and avoid capturing that place altogether. Yet no matter how you go about your search, it involves a journey.

Once you've found your home, one of the sweetest journeys is the one that brings you back, time and time again. Your home might be a fixed address. Or it might be the temporary quarters of a friend's guest room or high atop a mountain where a camp has been set up for the night. It's funny how quickly we can call a place home. It is as if the points of departure and arrival merge into one, embracing the long, extensive path we call our journey.

34 "Tell Me a Story"

"They may forget what you said, but they will never forget how you made them feel."
—CARL W. BUEHNER

HOW DO YOU TRULY MOVE ANOTHER HUMAN BEING? What do we have that's ours alone? Stories. Our life stories. The time your entire dinner burned up in smoke and the guests stayed anyway. That interview you clinched by just telling the truth about your previous job. A tale pieced together by a three-year-old who may never forget crawling around the front seat of the big, red fire truck.

Storytelling—and story listening—is one of the most powerful ways for people to connect and reconnect. The laughing and reminiscing are rich results that embed themselves into our memories, memories that often trigger smiles and comfort long after the story has been told.

As children, stories gave us our first impressions of what life could offer. In one night, you could be a firefighter, an inquisitive monkey, or a runaway bunny who knew he could always come home. Stories represented a world of possibilities, a universe that would not say no, a chance to escape into the lives of superheros, animals that could speak, and even furniture that had a point of view. And so for a short time—whether you sat in a circle on your kindergarten floor or snuggled perfectly into the arm of a grown-up who wanted nothing more than to be with you at that very moment—you could dream, forget where you were, and step into someone else's imagination. When we were kids, stories enabled us to temporarily leave the constricts of our Earth-bound existences. Like magic, words and pictures helped us make sense of our own lives—a frame of reference that we could accept or reject as impossible but wonderful nonetheless.

Stories make us feel OK when the universe seems a little out of whack. When we listen to a story, it's as if the camera in our mind's eye is zooming in, creating a close-up to block the troubles swirling around elsewhere. Stories validate our own lives—our fears, our joys, our sadness, our shaky faith in something or someone larger than life itself. When someone tells a story—regardless of the venue, whether it's a business meeting or two good friends huddled over their cups of coffee—a conversation begins.

Often, the conversation leaves a lasting impression. It's usually not the words that make an imprint but rather the facial expressions, the modulation of a voice. An excited voice may startle and be a little loud. Yet when that same voice speaks softly, even whispers, the message can be deafening. A story can lead to one of the best talks of your life.

This story has made a permanent home in my life. A few years ago, about a month before my father passed away, he told me a priceless tale. Before he married but after he'd come home from the army, he worked long hours at his own father's hardware store in Washington, D.C. Though I couldn't quite picture his youth, I could imagine the store, where I spent a lot of Saturdays scooping nails up from big, round bins and chewing Bazooka Bubble Gum. When he wasn't working, he played music. "I was one of a few in the union who could play tenor and alto sax," he said.

A bandleader who'd come to town knew a good thing and asked my father if he'd be interested in a seven-week gig. "The work was nightly, from 7:00 P.M. until 1:00 A.M.," he told me.

"Did you do it?" I asked, hoping desperately that he'd say yes.

"I did," he answered, "and I had the time of my life."

This story thrilled me. Here was a portion of his youth I'd never imagined. All at once the father who lay before me, losing the battle of a lifetime, became a man who tried on a dream. For seven weeks, he put in seventeen-hour days except on Sundays. At the end of the run, the bandleader asked my father if he'd go on the road.

"That would've meant 'good-bye hardware store,'" said my dad, with a crazy combination of regret and sense of obligation.

After that, we sat in silence for a while. In a terrifying flood of emotion, I was at once disappointed, saddened, and, strangely, thankful. My father was not what you'd call a go-getter, a career climber. Yet his flirtation with a dream engendered a respect I'd not felt before. And I loved opening that door to his past. Like a glimmer of light, I got the sense that my father may have truly understood some of my own disappointments and defeats. Later, after we had talked, I also felt a sense of forgiveness. What he could not give in the way of sympathy and support during my childhood, he expressed in a story near the end of his life.

Since that day I've often wondered what might have happened had he followed that bandleader, how different his life would have been. Each time, though, I shift back to the present and am thankful that for one afternoon he and I reconnected just because he had a story he needed to tell.

35 Play House

"Ah! there is nothing like staying at home, for real comfort."
—JANE AUSTEN, *EMMA* (1816)

HAVE YOU EVER HAD AN MMM, MMM GOOD peanut butter sandwich made by someone playing house? It's delicious, you know, and disappears from your hips just as fast as you can say, "Oh, that's good. May I have another?"

Playing house is a lovely reminder of how simple life can be with a few plastic utensils and some imagination. I clearly remember playing house as a child, but I played with real food. Like bread and water. Neither stained, and the rolled up pieces of Wonder Bread were as good then as M&Ms are today. Dabbling in domestic recreation didn't exactly prepare me for the real thing. But it did give me the chance to take a rest from the outdoors and actually connect, on my terms, with the home that gave me shelter.

Today, I don't think we play house enough. Even though more and more of us are doing things from home—ordering groceries, eating carryout, and watching HBO—we might still need a dose of a homegrown, traditional diversion—like preparing or attending a tea party, an essential and totally enjoyable form of playing house.

Like many of her peers, my daughter, at six, owned at least two tea sets. One contained about ten settings; the other, maybe six. But both included miniature teapots with matching cream and sugar sets. I usually provided store-bought or bakery-made cookies (or the rare homemade version), but nothing could satisfy her sweet tooth except the constant refilling of the thumb-sized container for sugar. Between the two of us, we made a colossal mess. Yet it is still one of my richest memories: her pretending to be a grown-up and me wanting to be a little girl again.

A few days ago I asked my friend Donna if she likes to play house. Not only did she know what I was talking about, but she raised a mutual concern. "I love to play house," she said. "But I like to bake when I play, and then I just eat what I've made." I was delighted that the spirit moves her but felt sorry that the end results prevented her from doing what she loves. I knew what she meant, though, because I do the same thing with slice after slice of home-made banana bread. So I did what any good friend would do: I offered to sit in her kitchen the next time she wants to play house. I'm a sucker for most home-baked goods anyway and did I mention that Donna has a new oven? Playing house is always fun; playing house with new appliances is sublime.

You can play house in a number of ways. Getting to know the four walls that surround you is a good place to start. Find a corner that engenders comfort and warmth and simply lounge about. Or add some whimsy to your game and set up a picnic in your living room. Or dust off the tea set that belonged to your grandma and host a party. If you live in a fixer-upper and possess the skills required to refurbish and remodel, visit your local home-improvement store. There you'll find the toys you need to play house with a purpose.

In the early years of my marriage, playing house took on an almost serendipitous flare. We had the requisite crates among our furnishings, and anything new seemed to glow for weeks before it finally began to blend into our surroundings. Yet the piece that still makes me smile was the mustard-colored laundry basket. Unlike the Holiday Inn end tables, the laundry basket served two purposes—a clothes hamper by day, a small table by night. Sometimes, that upturned laundry basket was set for two, and we'd dine on the floor of our bedroom (in the summer, it was the coolest room). These days, we keep most food out of our bedroom unless, of course, someone has brought me ice cream for breakfast.

Playing house can be as simple as doing something that puts you right back into your childhood. One woman I know swears by the restorative properties of sandwiches cut into triangular quarters. Someone else may revel in rearranging furniture.

In many ways, playing house as children involved role playing. Sometimes we played hospital, checking pulses and temperatures and then, with complete authority, dispensing medicine that tasted just like gum drops. Other times we constructed elaborate forts made of blankets and pillows. These were serious hideouts, after all.

Today you might play house by decorating for the holidays. Or you may set a table laden with all your finery for your favorite dinner guests. Like other rituals that bind us to our shelter, playing house may be one of the easiest ways to use your cherished past to create a more fulfilling present.

Beyond Shelter

When we take care of our homes, they take care of us. Here are some ways to give you and your home some loving care:

- Incorporate Feng Shui, the traditional Chinese art of cultivating spiritual power in your home by the strategic placement of certain objects.
- Begin a domestic dialogue. That's right, talk to your house. I do it all the time. Listen carefully and you might even hear something in return.
- Rearrange the furniture . . . as many times as you want.
- Get rid of what you don't use and what you don't need.

36 Five Minutes of Peace

"I never said 'I want to be alone,' I only said 'I want to be let alone.' There is all the difference."

—Greta Garbo, in John Bainbridge, *Garbo* (1955)

I KNOW A WOMAN WHO GETS UP REALLY EARLY in the morning. It's her alone time. She has three children, all under the age of five. So taking a few minutes for herself is the least she can do.

People of all ages need their peace. Kids find it in a crawl space under the stairs, deep inside a fort made of blankets and pillows, or in a treehouse that lifts them into their very own sanctuary. Sometimes we ask for our five minutes; sometimes we just take it where we can. It doesn't matter how or where you find your peace. What's important is that you make it a part of your everyday life.

As life becomes more crowded with obligations, those few minutes take on enormously rich proportions. Indeed, many people pay others to shop for their groceries, cut their lawns, and pick up and drop off their laundry, just so they'll have a little more free time. Yet for absolutely no charge you can catch your breath, get back on center, and maybe even think about something. All you need to do is stop what you're doing for five minutes.

There's a story I read to my kids about a wonderful mother elephant who wants just five minutes of peace from her active, though demanding, brood. But her plans to take an uninterrupted bath are thwarted over and over again. In the end, all three kids are in the tub with her, and instead of enjoying a good soak, she ends up with less than two minutes of peace.

Our moments of peace are like precious drops of rain in the midst of a drought. Whether you're in the car, on a bus or a train, or waiting in a doctor's office, you are entitled to simply take a few minutes to let your mind wander or think about something that has nothing to do with your commitments for the day. These few minutes are gifts. For me, they're like oxygen. In fact, when I remember, I take a few minutes to just breathe. If you've ever had to calm someone down, you probably said something like, "Breathe slowly; just take your time and breathe slowly." Think of the exercise instructor who reminds the class to "Breathe! Breathe!" It seems absurd that we forget to do the same for ourselves.

Just as we may forget to breathe, we may overlook the regenerative powers of alone time. Alone time—even five minutes out of a whole day—allows us to rediscover our spirit. Alone time causes us to be aware. It reminds us of who we are. In the midst of your alone time, you can exercise your senses. For instance, close your eyes and listen carefully to the sounds around you. The next day, sit outside and simply watch what's happening for a few minutes—leaves rustling, a squirrel pausing at the sound of a car.

It sounds so easy, doesn't it? After all, it's a narrow sliver of the day. Perhaps it's not the time involved but rather the idea of stopping. In some cases, though, doing nothing is better than doing something you don't want to do. Take the parenting concept called "time-out." The phrase entered my consciousness when my daughter was a toddler. Like a lot of parenting strategies, this one was begun with great hope. When my words became ineffectual, I'd plop her on the bottom step near the front hall and announce with my new-mother authority, "You're in time-out." Unfortunately, she was like one of those toys that you push down only to have it pop up again within a few seconds.

Clearly, this time-out thing wasn't working very well. But I needed to do something that would defuse the situation. So I began to give myself a time-out. I'd lock myself in the bathroom or go down to the basement. Sometimes my daughter would follow me around the house, adding to the lunacy. But those time-outs saved me. They still do. Taking five minutes to disarm my anger is one of the most effective ways for me to remain sane. More important, though, is the distance those moments create—distance that keeps my fury from bringing out the worst in me. Taking those five minutes allows me to bottle that fury, plug the bottle, and toss it out to sea. Invariably I feel better about myself. My kids win, too; instead of witnessing their mother transform into Medusa, they watch her disappear. And after five minutes of peace, I reappear, a little more composed, a little less anxious.

Count 1-2-3-4-5

Here are a few more ways to find five minutes of peace:

- Find a quiet corner in your home, a spot not normally for sitting but one where you might discover some peace.
- Before you crawl (or jump) out of bed in the morning, stay put and silently say good morning to the new day. Or sleep an extra five minutes. That's peaceful, too.

- Instead of tapping your foot and glancing at your watch at a busy check-out line, take the time to rest your head and let your mind wander.
- Next time you're doing the laundry, stand by the dryer for a few minutes and feel its heat and listen as the clothes turn over and over again.
- After you make your bed, lie down again without getting in.
- Hide out in your own house. Sometimes I hide in my closet when I absolutely, positively must be alone.

37 Scare Yourself Once in a While

"You must do the thing you think you cannot do."

—ELEANOR ROOSEVELT, *YOU LEARN BY LIVING* (1960)

SOME PEOPLE JUMP OUT OF AIRPLANES. Others climb the peaks of well-known mountains. I change the furnace filters and go sledding.

Why is fear so debilitating? And why, for goodness' sake, does it have such a wretched effect on our bodies—butterflies, shaky knees, a mysterious rash? Take the big, bad furnace in the basement. I don't know why, but every time I walk into the utility room, the hair on the back of my neck stands up on end. I start to sweat, and the responsibility of owning a house seems to eat me up.

Yet once I'm done slipping the dangerous furnace filter into its slot, I feel tremendously accomplished. In my own way, I give in to the fear. Denying it only feeds it and encourages its greedy appetite. Sometimes we're reluctant to face a fear and give it a name or shape. It's as if an admission of being frightened will set the fear and all that comes with it into motion. When we don't face our fears, we risk creating a big lie by telling ourselves we're not afraid. If you've ever done this, you know how much energy it takes to beat the fear into submission and bury it without destroying it.

When you scare yourself once in a while and give yourself permission to be afraid, it's a little easier for you and your fear to come face to face. When you face your fears, you may tremble. But it's possible to coexist with your fear. Instead of collapsing under a pair of wobbly knees, take that precarious feeling as a cue that you've got some work to do. Sometimes when we examine our fears—really undress them and have a nice, long look—we find they're a lot less powerful than we thought. It's like stepping into a prickly, muddy underbrush to retrieve a stray ball or anything that's rightly yours.

Brace yourself, take some precautions, and then do what you have to do. You may get a scratch or your head might ache a little. But that scuffle between you and your fear is over. You look around and see that you're still intact and the fear is gone or at least on its way. As kids, we did this constantly. Almost daily we faced one fear or another—the school-bus bully, the mysterious bump in the night, anything we couldn't control. Sometimes we would succumb, but in many cases we threw ourselves right into the middle of something completely scary. Otherwise, we knew we might miss whatever was ahead—something great, maybe even spectacular, like the most exhilarating roller coaster ride you had ever experienced.

Facing and overcoming your fears won't happen in an instant. Indeed, it could take years. But the only way to rein in your fears is to learn about them. Once you understand their origins, you can redirect the energy you've been using to fight them and free yourself to do the things that were locked up deep inside.

What emerges may truly be magnificent. You may discover, for example, that getting momentarily lost on a highway is not the end of the world. Or, after a few initial tumbles, you may become an avid fan of rollerblading. To those on the outside, it may not be much. What matters, though, is the smile on your own face when you look around, check things out, and then say out loud for everyone to hear, "I did it! I'm not afraid anymore!" This is the voice you want to hear—not the doubting banter that cajoles and pushes you away from what you really want.

Not long ago, I watched with awe as my daughter traveled up and down, from the bottom of a long flight of stairs to the top of a mountainous water slide. Over and over again, she slid down that winding, slippery path, always to the delight of her younger brother and to my utter astonishment. I wanted to experience her exhilaration but without the fear. I knew if I got to the top, I'd completely humiliate her by climbing down, defeated.

After pleading with me to follow her lead, I finally made my way up to the top. The lifeguard offered a few encouraging words, and I readied myself for the ride. I sat down, saw my life flash before me, and let go. I don't remember screaming, but when I landed in the pool I laughed and laughed. "I did it!" I cried to my girl, who this time was the one saying there was nothing to be afraid of. I took a few more runs and then settled back into a chair to watch my son test his own limits in the pool. And instead of looking up at that big water slide and seeing an insurmountable challenge, I saw the other things I might have to scare myself into doing, things I used to think I could not do.

38 Get Really Excited About the Little Things

"There are no little things. 'Little things,' so called, are the hinges of the universe."
—FANNY FERN, *GINGER-SNAPS* (1870)

LAST WEEK I BUMPED INTO A FRIEND who had recently completed her last round of chemotherapy. The first thing I noticed was her newly grown, beautiful head of hair. "Your hair looks great!" I told her.

She smiled and said, "I can put a comb through it."

I haven't stopped thinking about Cyndy and her comb. Even this morning as I rushed to pull a brush through my mass of wet tangles, I paused to remind myself of her recent triumph. Like the miracle of a newborn, the rebirth of Cyndy's multicolored locks—often a woman's most prized physical attribute—is cause for celebration.

I remember as a child getting really excited about what today may seem small potatoes. A new pair of shoes, for instance. At a very young age, I recall getting my first pair of shiny patent-leather Mary Janes. I wouldn't take them off the first day and happily spent the night wearing my new shoes. I probably wouldn't do that today, yet I wonder why we sometimes lose the capacity to get really excited about the little things as we get older. The big stuff—job promotions, the purchase of a home, a new romance—are natural causes for celebration and excitement. A positive reaction from those with whom we share our big news is almost guaranteed. But what about the little things, the smaller moments that add a little kick to our everyday lives?

Children have an enormous reservoir for simple enjoyment. They get excited over what we've long taken for granted: floating on your back, removing the training wheels once and for all, walking to the bus stop all alone. Kids show us how to value the impalpable, though dazzling, prizes we win when we get excited about the little things. Once we recognize the psychic payoff, the little things grow exponentially.

Later, when we celebrate the little things, we give ourselves a well-deserved and usually much-needed boost. Paying attention to life's intangible—though priceless—gifts teaches us about the things that really matter: a sympathetic glance from someone who's watching your toddler throw a tantrum, the embrace a friend gives because she knows how sad you're feeling, the unexpected card from someone in your past who just wanted to say hello. And then there are those moments that simply make life a little easier. Think of the jubilant feeling when, after several hours of darkness, your electricity suddenly returns after a particularly inconvenient blackout. Or the way you slip quickly into the perfect parking spot that would normally take an hour to find.

What little things do you get excited about? Maybe it's discovering a long-lost but never-forgotten earring that unexpectedly turns up under a chair. An out-of-the-blue telephone call from— or to—an old friend can give you a week's worth of emotional warmth and joy. An off-the-cuff remark you hear may become one of the most poignant observations you've encountered in a long time. Although these happenings may not evoke the same kind of jump-up-and-down excitement reminiscent of childhood, these experiences deserve our attention and thanks. Revel in them and keep looking for more.

We tend to notice the little things just when the big things either disappear or blow up before our very eyes. We tell ourselves and others, "Gee, this is when I really appreciate the smaller things in life." Somehow, though, we must try to disconnect that association and replace it with something more continuous, something more consistent, something we do every single day of the year. Our twenty-four-hour day provides ample opportunity to get excited about *something*. Starting today, try to find excitement in something you would otherwise overlook. Then use that excitement as currency to pay your way through the rest of the day. You may find that the more excited you become, the more exciting life will be.

It's All Relative

Some triumphs are inexplicable. You don't know why, but for some reason something small, something normally inconsequential, absolutely makes your day. Here are some small things that might get you really excited:

- Your newspaper publishes a recipe you've been looking for.
- Your hairdresser sends you home saying, "You still look fabulous! Don't come back for three weeks!"
- The wallpaper you've wanted to remove miraculously peels itself off.
- It happens: you get a flat tire, but you're prepared and you replace it with the spare with no problems.
- The jeans you thought you'd never get into suddenly fit fine.

39 Fill Your Toy Box

"It is in his pleasure that a man really lives; it is from his leisure that he constructs the true fabric of self."

—AGNES REPPLIER, *ESSAYS IN IDLENESS* (1893)

ABOUT A MONTH AGO I RECEIVED AN E-MAIL from a well-known Internet retailer. A $10 gift certificate was mine for the taking. I knew that I'd probably have trouble staying within the $10 limit and would, no doubt, have to subsidize the balance with my own money. Nonetheless, I enthusiastically clicked away as I began a little midday shopping spree.

As I perused the home page, one category practically jumped off the screen: toys for grown-ups. That's the one, I thought, as I started meandering through what turned into a delicious slide down memory lane.

Lite Brite, Twister, Clue, Operation. I fondly remembered each but happily settled for Clue. It arrived within about four days and sat for a few more on our front table. Suddenly, I wasn't so sure what to make of this nostalgic purchase. Perhaps I had reached some retro milestone. Maybe it was time for me to fill my toy box.

At my house, we are surrounded by wheels, marbles, assorted (and noisy) action figures, and other forms of entertainment. Like most parents, I am thrilled when my kids use their toys—even more so when they put them away, but that's another story. The point here is that the toys are *theirs*, not mine. So, once in a while, I want my own toys.

Why is play so elusive for some grown-ups? Because we are so strongly attracted and attached to a profoundly goal-oriented, work-ethic-driven society. Like other forms of nonwork, play connotes wastefulness, a stoppage in the way of what needs to get done. Yet often what really needs to get done has more to do with our hearts and spirits and less to do with a deadline or longstanding project. Play beckons to us, urging us to live in the present moment, a moment that becomes more luminous when we disallow interruptions like work and worry.

We can enlarge the moment even more by setting aside the rules we learned so well and so long ago. Watch kids play a game and you're likely to witness a group enamored with—indeed, dependent upon—a well-established set of rules. Games with rules provide a sense of order, a notion of what's fair and right. Rules give kids a chance to win. As we get older, though, we learn how to play without necessarily having to win. When we can shelve the rules for a bit and forfeit that need to succeed over someone else's failure, we give ourselves the chance to enjoy a moment of bliss all by ourselves.

I know someone whose bliss includes some nylon and string. A couple of years ago, when visiting my friends Phyllis and Scott, I marveled over Scott's childlike anticipation as he opened a box that had been delivered while he worked hard at his day job. "It's the kite!" he exclaimed. His contagious joy and complete thrill over the arrival of his latest toy reminded me, in such a poignant way, of how important it is to play. In that short period of time, as Scott opened the package, I learned a lot about kites—some have more than one line and even the lines themselves are made of different materials. But what has stayed with me most is the elation Scott wore on his face and the excitement I heard in his voice.

Someone else I know keeps his toy box in the kitchen. He is a chef and a host in his own home, always preparing a bounty that is both beautiful and appetizing. Whenever I'm in that kitchen, I stare at his collection of pots and pans that are suspended like a Calder mobile from the ceiling. The food he creates is a gastronomical gift, but the tools he uses are as much a part of his art as the pièce de résistance that eventually finds its way to the table. "It's my playroom, my domain," he says.

Filling your toy box should be stress free, without the anxiety associated with obtaining the best, the latest, the most technologically advanced gizmo on the market. An audiotape or CD of your favorite comedian played in your car during a two-hour commute may be all you need to start your collection. An action figure sitting on your bookshelf or desk at work can be inspiring and playful at the same time. And if anyone ever says, "Oh, go fly a kite!" consider answering with "That's a great idea! I think I will."

40 "Can You Come Out and Play?"

"Each friend represents a world in us, a world possibly not born until they arrive, and it is only by this meeting that a new world is born."

—ANAÏS NIN, *THE DIARY OF ANAÏS NIN*, VOLUME 2 (1967)

WHEN I WAS GROWING UP, I played outside for hours. I'd roller-skate, ride my bike, play games with other kids, or just walk up and down the street and talk to anybody willing to listen. Entire afternoons sped by, one after the other, like planes on a busy runway. We took our time, but we hurried, too, because we wanted to get as much play out of our days as possible. Our friendships depended on it.

In most cases, what we accomplished outside and in each other's homes all started because someone asked the best question of all: "Can you come out and play?" Kids didn't have play dates back then. Usually, you'd just ring someone's doorbell, walk through the front hall, and see what was up. Maybe you played "kick the can" and "dodgeball." Or perhaps you built forts and then hid out for hours. Water fights and spying were fun, too. One of my most memorable adventures is one that my childhood friend Carole and I still talk about. Unless it's been unearthed, a

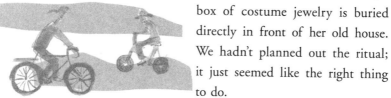

box of costume jewelry is buried directly in front of her old house. We hadn't planned out the ritual; it just seemed like the right thing to do.

Today it's not always easy to go out with our friends to play. If you plan something, you risk getting bumped by something else. Yet a spontaneous get-together seems equally out of reach. In many ways, "Can you come out and play?" has been replaced with "I'd like to get together, but I have too much to do, so let's look at our calendars next week. . . ." Still, some of my favorite recent memories are the ones that have come about because someone turned a "maybe" into a sure thing.

Most of our lives are brimming over with carpools, full- and part-time jobs, and deciding what to have for dinner. We're always trying to catch our breath. Unfortunately, our attempt to balance work and family doesn't always include our friends. Not only might they take a backseat, they may have to ride in another car altogether. How did our friends become a casualty in our struggle to keep our lives glued together?

Some of us feel guilty at the thought of leaving our kids with a sitter to spend time with a friend—especially if we've been apart all day. For a lot of people, leisure continues to get bumped as work becomes more and more demanding. After all, in the abstract, it's a lot easier to give up time with friends than time on the job or with your family. Eventually, though, we feel the impact of such neglect. And contrary to some conventional wisdom, you can't always pick up where you left off.

On the other hand, some friendships flourish under these conditions. I have collected friends over a lifetime, friends who may not know what movies I've seen (not many) or even the length of my hair. But they know other things, things that transcend the miles that separate us and the years that compose our history. When I recently returned to my hometown for a short visit, I wrapped my weekend with some time with old friends. No one had advance notice, but we still got to reconnect.

Making time for your friends shouldn't be taxing. But it does take a little work. If you're separated by distance, plan a weekend together. You can alternately visit one another or meet halfway. Carve out time for your good friends' birthdays and celebrate. Form a book group with your reading friends. If you haven't heard from a friend, call her up and ask how she's doing. It may be just the catalyst you need to reignite a friendship. Steal time whenever you can. You'll cherish these moments for years to come.

41 Hit the Ground Running

"Life engenders life. Energy creates energy. It is by spending oneself that one becomes rich."

—Sarah Bernhardt, in Cornelia Otis Skinner, *Madame Sarah* (1966)

Recently, my son discovered the pure joy of swinging a bat into an oncoming ball. Once he hears the cracking sound of the stick meeting the sphere—followed by the screeching of his fans to "Run!!"—he demonstrates a most amazing feat: a driven human spirit.

For our homegrown baseball diamond, we generally rely on Mother Nature or miscellaneous items to provide the bases and home plate—a bush, a horseshoe, a Frisbee, a mound of grass. But he dismisses these markers for an alternative journey. After my young slugger hits the ball, he thrusts one fist toward the sky with a proud and resounding, "Yes!" followed by his urge to hit the ground running. He begins the circuitous route around the bases at breakneck speed. Sensing the thrill of triumph and soaking in the loud and steady affirmation from friends and family, he reaches into the spotlight for a generous slice of baseball glory.

Do the bases restrict his movements? Of course not; he seeks a larger moment—indeed, a *longer* moment.

This home movie isn't recorded on tape. It's in my head, and I play it over and over, especially when I contemplate a new beginning. What makes this scene so memorable is my son's—and most children's—ability to react to an immediate desire or instinct. My son does not analyze. He does not think. If he does, he may not take the journey. Instead, he tears ahead, circling a bush ten times his size, unwinding like a top, then dashing diagonally across our neighbor's front yard. For a few seconds he ducks around the corner of our house, then he reappears for a final and victorious grand-slam trip home.

My son's exhilaration—his complete pride—reminds me of our own potential to touch life's infinite and simple joys. His movements and his expressions tell the world, "I'm achieving something and I feel good about it!" At six, he is able to strike a balance between pride and showmanship. Achieving that balance as an adult becomes a little more complicated. Yet we, too, are capable of great, soulful riches if, like my son, we can hit the ground running.

As adults, we tend to overthink and overanalyze. We also forget to pay attention. Before we know it, an opportunity is gone. A friend gets tired of waiting for you to respond to an invitation. Your child's impromptu, after-dinner performance can't compete with your need to clean up the kitchen.

In the business world, opportunities come and go in a heartbeat. Take the case of a business start-up. The first advice? Write a business plan. My guess, however, is that a lot of successful start-ups are still around because the founders were too busy working to stop and compose a full-fledged business plan.

Certainly, careful examination is essential in many situations. But it's not always possible to know what's around the next corner. Even the imperfect unknown can be edited once it begins to take form. Therein lies the serendipitous nature of risk. Betting on the stock market poses all sorts of possible losses. Yet investors often risk losing out on big wins if they stay behind.

For many people, jumping (or gingerly stepping) into the unknown is fraught with peril. "What if? . . ." "What happens when? . . ." "I can't imagine." Anxiety begins to fiercely compete with hope. Uncertainty becomes an all-encompassing scary reality.

Yet uncertainty doesn't have to be bad. Uncertainty is often just a blanket covering wonderful possibilities. Think of a relationship. Have you ever met someone and immediately felt a bond? A shared interest or experience can fast-forward a friendship into something that, in other circumstances, could take years. Trust, for instance, has a long growing season. But what if your instincts say to you, "I think I can trust this person," not long after an introduction? Do you accept your instincts and take the risk? Or do you hear a cautious voice say, "Don't do it"?

Whether it's a relationship or an idea, holding back may lead to regrets and misgivings. It's easy to walk away from the unknown. But as comfortable as it may feel to be risk-free, the loss of what could be something wonderful and exciting can leave you empty and unfulfilled. Anyone can make a list of all the good reasons for *not* doing something. Indeed, how can the comfort of the familiar possibly compete with the uneasiness associated with unexplored terrain?

Whether it's your dream business or the person of your dreams, a swing at home plate or a chance to go home again, consider—even for a minute—the galaxy of possibilities. Try to get comfortable with what you don't know. In other words, when the spirit moves you, run with it, regardless of what "it" may be.

42 Dress Up

"I know you! Your motto is 'Silk socks and dubious feet.'"

—COLETTE, *THE OTHER ONE* (1929)

WHEN I WAS GROWING UP, my bedroom had two closets. One held my jumpers, skirts, blouses, and other juvenile threads. The other served as storage for my mother's out-of-season wardrobe, which included a luxurious fur coat. I never actually removed the coat from its hanger, but very often I would encircle myself within its satiny interior and then brush my nose into the smooth and warm fur.

The thrill of secretly opening that closet door and imagining myself wearing something so marvelous is my first memory of playing dress up. Next, I discovered her jewelry. Some pieces were locked in what I recall were beautiful cloth-covered boxes, but most I could reach and drape over my neck. I felt like a princess.

As little girls, our dress-up days made us feel good about ourselves. And although we thought of it as play, dressing up was really one of our first experiences at building our self-esteem. "Do you like my hair?" "Where *did* you get that dress?" Between our fashion banter and changing from one outfit to another, entire afternoons would go by before we had to put on our "real" clothes. And even if we never checked ourselves out in a full-length mirror, we knew we looked beautiful because we *felt* beautiful.

Though our dress-up days are over, we can still reclaim that special feeling that came over us when we slipped into our mother's high-heeled shoes. Whether you're commuting to a job downtown or getting comfortable in your home office, dressing up can add some zest to your day. Perhaps you're just running out to the store to buy your weekly groceries. It may not be a special occasion, but it's still an event. There's no rule that says you can't dress up to buy a quart of milk (but if there were such a rule, I'd heartily recommend that you break it!).

In our casual-chic society, we just don't have as many opportunities to dress up as we used to. Remember when flying meant more formal attire? Those days are over, yet we still like to step out and show off our wardrobes. Think of someone you know who always looks put together. She probably adds a little color to her outfit and wears accessories particularly well. See if you can emulate a little of her style to infuse some pizzazz into your own appearance. If you don't know where to start, ask for her advice. She'll be flattered and will want to help you achieve your goal.

Sometimes we need to dress up because we're feeling less than who we actually are. I call that *schlumpy*. Schlumpy is when you catch your reflection in a store window, and you want to dive into the nearest fountain. Schlumpy is when you feel bloated and can't breathe in your favorite jeans. Schlumpy is when a bad hair day doesn't begin to explain the troubles you're having.

Dressing up lets the world know where you stand when it comes to fashion. Adding a scarf or a headband to your ensemble will go a long way toward pulling it all together. Dressing up is also a great way to pretend you've got a savvy sense of fashion. All you need, really, is one outfit that gets out once in a while. If you do need a little guidance, consider tapping one of the many retailers that offer one-on-one fashion counseling. You'll leave the store a little poorer, but you will probably have made a sound investment—not just in the clothes, but, more important, in yourself. Finally, remember two things: first, fluorescent lighting has no redeeming qualities; and two, fads are not necessarily a bad thing—they fly in the face of rules, which means you'll probably have fun wearing the latest thing.

A Red Hat

A little dress up—a mere accessory—can go a long way. But as we progress through the years, many of us are blessed with the knowledge that beauty truly does come from within. The following, which has been circulating on the Internet, says it best:

A Woman's Viewpoint

Age 8: looks at herself and sees Cinderella

Age 15: looks at herself and sees Cinderella/Sleeping Beauty/cheerleader

Age 20: looks at herself and sees too fat/too thin, too short/too tall, too straight/too curly, decides she doesn't have time to fix it and goes out

Age 40: looks at herself and sees too fat/too thin, too short/too tall, too straight/too curly and says, "At least I'm clean," and goes out

Age 50: looks at herself, says "I am," and goes wherever she wants to

Age 60: looks at herself and remembers all the people who can't even see themselves in the mirror anymore; goes out and conquers

Age 70: looks at herself, sees wisdom and laughter, and goes out to enjoy life

Age 80: doesn't even bother to look; just puts on a red hat and goes out to be who she is

43 "Pick Me Up!"

"Those whom we support hold us up in life."

—MARIE VON EBNER-ESCHENBACH, *APHORISMS* (1893)

TOWARD THE END OF A LONG DAY, my son occasionally wanders into the kitchen where I am usually simultaneously preparing dinner, cleaning up from breakfast, and declining a telemarketer's fabulous offer. He makes his way over to my center of gravity with outstretched arms and eyes that seem to say, "Pick me up." I adore this plea for connection. It's an excuse to stop what I'm doing and feel the rich and warm touch of someone who means more to me than life.

I marvel at the ease with which he comes to me for support. With no words, he seeks sustenance and receives it, reminding me for a split second of how breast-feeding sustained us both through his first year of life. His quiet quest for a break from his daily grind also prods my mind toward a vexing question: as we grow older, why does it become so hard to ask for support when we need it most?

As children, we were, for the most part, protected from the stigma that often accompanied an appeal for help and comfort. But as adults we're more exposed; expressing our need for support is somehow interpreted as a sign of weakness, an admission that once in a while we need a little help. I'm not talking about the event planner who must delegate responsibilities to her team or the general contractor who is paid to keep things rolling during the construction of a new home. I'm talking about our everyday selves, the ones who seem to relish each and every straw that can be thrown upon the camel's back. We're usually not thinking about the proverbial last straw; we're just intent upon heaping on as many as we can. Well, that last straw eventually reaches its target. By that time, our backs are hurting awfully bad and we could use a little support.

Are we afraid of showing weakness in these self-sufficient times? Are we concerned about how others will perceive us? Will we be expected to reciprocate? Heaven knows, our need to rely on others is universal. What's not so common, however, is our ability to take the next step and ask to be held. Few of us want to be known for being needy. But there's a difference between neediness and just needing some support once in a while.

Certainly, the circumstances surrounding our moments of need vary and may even seem unsavory. Perhaps you've made an error in judgment and need to vent your regrets before actually repairing any damage. Maybe an unpleasant experience has chipped away at the thick shell you have so carefully built over the course of a lifetime. Regressing to childish feelings—and even childish behavior—happens to more people than you think.

So how do we ask for help? How do we communicate our need to be picked up and held? It begins with someone we can trust. The people we trust are more than mere listeners. These are the people who become our refuge, who shelter us from the storms that occasionally try to swallow us whole. Think of someone who's leaned on your shoulder in the past, and lean on her. At first, you may shrink at switching roles with a person who at one point stood with wobbly knees and a shaken heart. But isn't this one of the extraordinary privileges of being a friend anyway? And remember, too, that no one is immune from hard times. Sure, everything is relative and one person's bad luck may be another person's minor inconvenience. Yet if we're talking about the people who you're close to, then you probably have a few choices—choices who, if called upon, would step up to the plate and swing on your behalf.

Don't think of your request as a deficit. Think of your search and discovery as part of the circle of compassion. You may find a truly empathetic set of ears. Or two eyes that simply absorb the suffering that cannot be expressed. Compassion is both teacher and student. When we show it, we teach it to others. When we feel it, we learn how it heals.

If someone approaches you with outstretched arms, accept the invitation with grace, and consider yourself part of the same chain that holds and supports but hangs on for dear life as well.

Learn How to Ask

Asking for support takes practice. Here are some ways to seek out support:

- Call or E-mail a friend and, unabashedly, ask for help. Also, tell this person how much you appreciate her or his time.
- If you're feeling squeezed by your family, tell them so. Give everyone specific ideas on how they can help.
- Accept a friend's invitation to visit or to be taken out to dinner.
- Forget about asking and just call a trusted friend to cry. She or he will know what to do.

44 Trick or Treat

"I change myself, I change the world."

—GLORIA ANZALDUA, *BORDERLANDS/LA FRONTERA* (1987)

THE SWEET AROMA OF HALLOWEEN CANDY is in a category of its own. Ever since I can remember, the arrival of those once-yearly pound bags of Baby Ruths, Nestlé Crunches, and other assorted confections marked the countdown of what is still one of my favorite celebrations of the year.

If you share my fondness for this autumnal fete, then you already know how good it feels to inhale the scent of pure sugar as it commingles with the crispness of October's last evening. Even if candy isn't your thing, the night is not without possibilities.

What makes Halloween so appealing? It's simple: dress up, trickery, and, of course, treats. But there's no reason to wait 365 days to indulge in a little mischief and whimsy. We could all probably use a little "Boo!" in our lives. Injecting some "let's pretend" into our otherwise normal routine also lets us set aside the way-too-serious nature of things. We get to let our hair down (or perhaps put our hair under a funky wig). We're given a chance to act like something we're not. Think of the little boy dressed up as Superman who runs from house to house crying, "I can fly! I can fly!" or the young girl dressed up as a princess who walks as if she's greeting all her subjects.

Halloween's greatest gift is its simple fun. Enjoy it year-round. If you're feeling devilish in February, slip on a pair of leopard print gloves to keep the cold at bay. In the summer, throw a garden party with a special theme—select a decade and ask your guests to arrive in costumes from that period. If traffic jams are getting you down, keep a clown nose in the glove compartment and use it. It'll be your way of showing the world that you know how to have a good time, anywhere. You might even lighten the load of the guy looking at you in his rearview mirror.

Whether it's a new nose or a full-fledged costume, exchanging our regular garb for something totally different lets us be a stranger—to others and to ourselves. The idea is to borrow a little bit of the exhilaration and release that Halloween delivers year after year. For instance, think of the Elvira-inspired wig—long, stringy black hair—that gives one a totally different look. A new haircut in the middle of the year might just give you and others a little jolt. Sometimes that little shock is all that's needed to lift us out of an inexplicable ennui. Have you ever felt as if your life is progressing along a flat line though the peaks and valleys are what you truly crave? If, like me, you occasionally long for a new role to play, consider the bewitching and haunting nature of Halloween.

You may not spot the Great Pumpkin or hear a bat flapping around your attic. But who's to stop you from enjoying a little mischief?

45 Don't Clean Your Room

"Housekeeping is like being caught in a revolving door."
—MARCELENE COX, IN *LADIES' HOME JOURNAL* (1944)

AS A YOUNG GIRL, nothing brought me greater serenity than having a clean room. No dirty clothes hiding in a corner. Dolls neatly resting—shoulder to shoulder—on my bookshelf. Hospital-cornered bed made every day (even on sick days).

I don't know if my tidiness was born out of a need to please my mother, who's very organized, or my own attachment—at the time—to order and the absence of clutter. I do know, however, that at some point between my departure from home and where I live today, having a place for everything lost its meaning or, at the very least, is simply not as important as it used to be. Other pursuits beckon. Like checking out a new website or looking for a stray sock. Anything, really, that comes to mind.

Perhaps I am making up for lost time. Most kids tend to leave things on their bedrooms' floors, buried deep under a bed, or in a closet corner. My daughter claims to feel a sense of comfort by the haphazard placement throughout her room of all that she owns. "There are too many other fun things to do," she says.

I tend to agree. What exactly is so sinister about incurring a little mess in our lives anyway? Many of us lose our precious equilibrium over areas of our lives that for one reason or another are just a bit untidy. The pressure to clean and the guilt for not doing it fast enough are ridiculous. Sometimes I even leave a few dirty dishes in the sink *just because I can*. These days I'm paying less attention to the barely visible ring around the tub and dust bunnies marking time and focusing more on the things that really matter—legendary skies that look like watercolor masterpieces right outside our front door, impromptu concerts by my kids, a telephone conversation that requires my undivided attention.

As a kid, maybe you were opposed to cleaning your room. Or, cleaning up was held as collateral for what you really wanted to do. It's not surprising that we carry those feelings over into adulthood. Yet, as a grown-up, the consequences for not cleaning your room aren't nearly as severe as they once were. You'll probably still have dessert after dinner, and you may even get that new toy you've been wanting.

And as much as I plead with my daughter to clean her room, I know that her tendency toward untidiness offers a flip side. It is a sign that life is tugging on her sleeve as she takes that extraordinary and meteoric journey toward adolescence. Unlike me when I was her age, her sense of order has less to do with the placement of dolls and more to do with what the universe has to offer. And although my exasperation occasionally reaches off-the-scale levels, I find that what we may not share in our respective childhoods, we see perfectly eye to eye on in our parallel lives today.

If the universe is calling you, don't clean your room. Because as many moments as there are in the universe, most of the good ones are short-lived and are gone before you know it. A mess, on the other hand, will almost always be waiting.

Portable Chaos

When I'm feeling especially unhinged, on the brink of total chaos, I clean out my purse. If you don't carry a purse, you can always substitute by cleaning out an over-the-top junk drawer. I don't know about you, but sometimes my bag becomes one oppressive cornucopia of receipts, extra napkins, hide-the-evidence candy wrappers, and other small scraps of my yesterdays. Purging these extras eventually becomes something I look forward to. The best way to start is to simply turn your bag upside down and shake out the contents with no fear about what might tumble out—an unpaid bill, for instance, or even a half-eaten cookie.

What's so appealing about this monthly ritual? Well, the sheer weight of the collection of trash is mind-boggling. Plus, for a little while anyway, you can actually reach inside without looking and pull out what you need without a struggle—a simple though tremendously satisfying feeling. What is probably most extraordinary is how positively peaceful this whole process can make you feel. In some ways, my purse is an extension of my brain. In a week's time, my purse becomes a filing cabinet with virtual folders that tell me what I've spent, where I've been, and what I still need to do. When I clear all that out, my head benefits, too.

46 Take a Nap

"Sleep was her fetish, panacea and art."
—MARY WEBB, GONE TO EARTH (1917)

I OFTEN HEAR MOTHERS REMARK that their children have given up their naps. They usually share this news with a sense of surrender and anxiety. After all, it's hard to regulate a child's sleep patterns. And no matter how natural it is for a child to eliminate a midday rest, the loss of a nap is a major milestone for everyone. It's especially daunting for a mom who has come to rely upon a brief respite—an hour or so during which she's not focusing her attention solely on her child.

My friend Susan, mother of four and nap aficionada, says that when a child gives up her nap she is making a statement about growing up and getting on with her life. When adults take a nap, we do so not as a regression, but rather as a way to pace ourselves, replenish ourselves, and do what it takes to avoid burnout. Burnout is not restricted to the burden of one job or a longstanding, toxic relationship. Burnout can happen when you've dried the last dish and it's after 11 P.M. or on the fifth day in a row that you've been late for work. A midweek nap or a quick rest on a Sunday afternoon may be the antidote you've been looking for.

Ironically, both the child and the adult responses are expressions of independence. A child says, "I'm not tired! I want to play!" An adult says, "I'm tired! I don't want to play [work] anymore!"

I have a theory about naps. I believe that after many years, we realize—usually in the middle of a particularly exhausting and vexing day—that somehow our right to nap has simply disappeared, not unlike our custom to have milk and cookies in the late afternoon.

What happened here? Some of us might feel a little guilty for wanting something that society has deemed unnecessary and even excessive and extravagant (and what's wrong with *that*, anyway?). We're also not very good at accepting fatigue, as if admitting that you're exhausted is some dreadful confession.

It's truly amazing what we can withstand and how far we can run when we have *a lot to do*. People, women in particular, have an irrational fear that if we momentarily stop and regroup and reenergize, we'll never build up to the energy we had before, as if some kind of atrophy will set in. In our gotta-go-here, gotta-do-that way of life, slowing down to take a rest seems wasteful. It's as if the whole kingdom will come to a standstill for a hundred years if we allow our eyes to close in the middle of the day.

Don't think of rest as giving in. Rather, consider a nap, or even closing your eyes for five minutes, as something you've worked hard for, something you've earned, like the interest in a bank account. Instead of banishing the nap, try to find ways to comfortably fold it into your life. View the nap as you might perceive vitamins and exercise. Remove words like *slothful* and *lazy* from your nap vocabulary. Replace them with declarations like "Naps are good for my soul" and "A little rest will make me feel like a million bucks."

The benefits of napping are numerous. Dreaming in the middle of day, for example, is one of the best ways to escape the all-too-much moments that threaten to put us over the edge. Even corporate America has discovered the benefits of allowing employees a few Zs on the job. Indeed, some companies encourage the power nap versus the power lunch. Resting your head on your desk no longer means you're bored; you may simply need to restore your energy. In fact, a quick snooze can boost your alertness and awaken your creativity.

Usually, babies and children are coerced into taking their naps. In fact, I cannot think of a time when I heard a three-year-old announce that it was nap time. But don't let the absence of that "time to nap" voice prevent you from taking a well-needed rest. You can nap anywhere—as you wait to board a plane, on the plane itself, in the carpool line, on the floor behind your desk (you can always close the door), in the passenger seat of a car, on the subway or bus, and, of course, in your favorite chair. If necessary, count a few sheep or iguanas—it doesn't matter—to get you closer to the druglike freefall that occurs when we leave our waking selves and enter the Land of Nod. It is pure heaven on Earth.

47 Make a Wish

"Star light, star bright.

First star I see tonight.

Wish I may, wish I might

Have the wish I wish tonight."

—TRADITIONAL CHILDREN'S NURSERY RHYME

DO YOU SAVE THE WISHBONE? Do you pause before you blow out the candles? Does wishing make it so?

I don't remember exactly where or when I witnessed my first shooting star. I do know, however, that ever since I've always made a point of making a wish on that meteoric miracle. And why not? Just as we are free to believe, we are equally entitled to make wishes and dream.

What did you used to wish for? A snow day? Five snow days in a row? How about wishing for three more wishes? It didn't matter what you wished for. What mattered was that you could wish for anything. Some kids wish they could fly. They may never actually grow wings, but some of those big dreamers grow up to become pilots and astronauts. Other children wish with all their hearts for things closer to home, like not having to share a bedroom. They may have to wait, but sometimes an older sibling who goes off to college gives new meaning to having a room of one's own. I know kids who wish birthdays came more than once a year. Who's to say we can't celebrate our half birthdays? With some cake, a few candles, and a present or two, this is a wish that *can* come true.

A lot of us have to-do lists, but how many of us have wish lists? Not the kind that your favorite shop keeps on file but the one that no one ever sees, the one you hold onto like a child who clutches a beloved blanket. Sometimes our wishes seem so extraordinary, we wouldn't dream of putting them on such a list. That will never happen, you may say to yourself. Or, don't be ridiculous; wishes don't come true.

Unfortunately, as we get older, reason and logic push wishes and dreams to the side. It's as if adulthood pulls the whimsy right out from under our noses. Yet most people who accomplish the seemingly impossible are quick to point out that sometimes dreams really do come true. Think of the difference between moving mountains and *believing* in moving mountains. That will is not unlike the famous train who thought it could and, finally, did get over the mountain. The trains that came before didn't believe it was possible to get to the other side.

Sometimes we turn to wishing because we think that's the only way we'll get through. What before was a childhood perk—a special bonus just for kids—turns into a method of survival, a way to cope with what we can't understand or control. Sometimes we wish for others, especially when we see no other way to offer help. If you dream about something coming true, it's a kind of wish fulfillment. And even then, that may be all we have.

What I've learned is that the rate at which wishes do come true is directly related to our willingness to believe. If you don't believe, you're unlikely to make a connection between the good things in life and your expression of faith. Think about what you're wishing for. Can you combine your will with a plan to make your wish come true? Can you simply make up your mind to believe in what you cannot see, what cannot be proved? Sometimes, all we have is our heart and soul and an intangible hunch that something bigger is at work, something we can't possibly imagine.

This impalpable grip we have on what may or may not be is immensely powerful. It's what keeps the budding politician focused on her dream to become president. It's what sustains the struggling actor who occasionally imagines his name on the marquee. It's what carries the Little Leaguer all the way to home plate as he imagines himself a hero at the World Series.

My friend Mary Ellen is good at replenishing her wish list. She's also quick to poke holes in the philosophy that warns us to be careful what we wish for. "That's a curse!" she exclaimed one day. "If you go into the jungle looking for tigers, you might find them." In other words, great achievements often involve great risk. And while we should take care not to wish for what may not be good for

Star light, star bright.
First star I see tonight.
Wish I may, wish I might
Have the wish I wish tonight.

us, neither should we be afraid to have big dreams. If Mary Ellen's wish doesn't come true or it takes a wrong turn, she simply makes another wish. That's the nice thing about wish lists: you can always add one more thing. Whether you wish on an eyclash, a wishbone, or a dandelion, just remember that no one can be absolutely sure about its outcome. And if your wish just happens to come true, don't forget to thank your lucky stars.

Wishful Thinking

On every night, nearly five billion shooting stars fall through the sky. If you happen to see one, consider making a wish. Here are a few ideas:

- I wish I could fly.
- I wish my dog would stop barking.
- I wish someone else would make dinner for a week.
- I wish ice cream had no calories.
- I wish I could sleep late.
- I wish I could be in a movie.
- I wish for a four-day work week.
- I wish the word *impossible* would disappear.
- I wish I made a bazillion bucks.
- I wish my house could clean itself.

48 Dawdle

"There is no pleasure in having nothing to do; the fun is in having lots to do and not doing it."

—MARY WILSON LITTLE, *A PARAGRAPHER'S REVERIES* (1904)

WHEN I WAS SMALL, but old enough to have a watch and tell the time, I cultivated one of humankind's most precious pastimes—dawdling. Lingering over a flower (and occasionally picking it and running home), walking the length of a neighbor's brick wall one more time, or just talking with a friend were the crown jewels of my days spent outdoors.

Yet how many of us were admonished with the words, "Don't dawdle!"? What could possibly be so bad about wasting a little time? Well, it must have been something quite threatening, because many cultures are still quick to minimize and even abolish what is really an innocuous form of simple pleasure.

I'm not advocating something dangerous, such as encouraging an emergency-room staff to slow down. I am defending, however, the universal need to, say, get sucked in by the cheesy cable movie rather than going grocery shopping or getting to the bank before closing time. A lot of self-help books encourage readers to slow down, take it easy, smell the roses, and generally live in the present moment. Perhaps this advice is difficult to follow because we're not sure of the payoff.

Dawdling is different. The possibilities for a rich payoff are boundless. Let's look at the weekend. The mountain of circulars found in most Sunday papers is fertile ground for what could turn into fruitful dawdling. So you weren't exactly in the market for a bread maker, but one store's deal has that machine on your kitchen counter faster than you can eat a slice of homemade rye.

Dawdling, idling, procrastinating—they're all wonderful ways to *avoid*. Sometimes we absolutely must avoid starting or completing certain tasks. If you're not in abject pain, putting off a root canal is not such a bad thing. And if you're the industrious type, your dawdling and procrastination may lead to completing other projects that you've ignored. When I don't want to write (but have a looming deadline), I make an effort to organize my office or run out to buy a birthday card.

Dawdling can build character. My daughter recently asked for the eighteenth time if she could get off the school bus at the first stop in the neighborhood. I had said no for nearly a year but knew that her independence was crying to be set free. The peace of mind of seeing one's child hop off the bus right in front of your house is not a concept easily embraced by a young child who wants to grow up fast. So I relented, and each day from 3:30 P.M. until I see her walking down the street or bolting through the garage door, my heart beats a little faster and my imagination wanders into fearful territory. And though one day she confessed to dawdling, I rejoiced inside, remembering the solitary joys I once experienced around the same age.

Dawdling can lead to great discoveries. I have a scene in mind. My friend Chris had promised to find me a certain pithy quotation by Shakespeare, one I planned to include in this book. She was moving, however, and hoped to find the quote among papers as she boxed up her belongings. Naturally, I encouraged her to pace herself in a way that is consistent with successful dawdling. That is, one must slow down to find something long since lost. Happily, Chris found the quote, and we both rejoiced in her discovery.

Self-discovery is another wonderful benefit associated with doing anything other than what we're supposed to be doing. Sometimes when I'm rifling through one of my numerous (and now famous, I believe) piles of paper, I stumble upon a really bad piece of writing penned by yours truly. I stop what I'm doing and reread something awful that actually inspires hope and renewal. I can become better at this, I say to myself. More important, though, is the sliverish glance I get of my past, of the way I was thinking when I was twenty or sixteen. For some reason, this makes me feel whole and reminds me that my life is really a journey that is neither static nor without wonderful possibilities.

Dawdling allows us to accidentally stumble upon ourselves. When we trip on something, we usually slow down for a moment to look around and find the source of our fall. Often, when we slow down we also take some time to reflect. It might be a tangent, something far from where we were a moment earlier, but imagine how far you can go if you give in to your instincts to dally and, in general, step around the "have to's" and "should's."

I am convinced that there are times in everybody's experience when there is so much to be done, that the only way to do it is to sit down and do nothing.

—FANNY FERN, FOLLY AS IT FLIES (1868)

49 Put on Your Thinking Cap

"Never be afraid to sit awhile and think."

—LORRAINE HANSBERRY, *A RAISIN IN THE SUN* (1959)

WHEN A TEACHER INSTRUCTED US TO "Put on our thinking caps," almost everyone followed her lead by placing imaginary hats upon our heads, then tying them securely beneath our chins. We'd been given a problem or asked a question and now it was time to get serious—our cue to focus and set aside the usual distractions. It was as if our caps held all the answers we'd ever need, at least until the bell rang. Our thinking caps gave us the freedom to formulate our opinions instead of simply spitting out the first things that came to mind.

Over time, we grow out of our thinking caps. We're pushed by others and ourselves to act before we've had a chance to ruminate, to test a decision and weigh the consequences. This isn't to say that giving in to our spontaneous instincts is bad. Indeed that is, in part, the spirit behind these pages. Yet when we want to think and we're not allowed, or we don't give ourselves the time, we shortchange ourselves and then later wonder why we didn't give something more thought. Just when it's really important to take a minute to reflect, you've got to run for the train, offer a succinct opinion at a business meeting, or agree to something you're regretting before the words even leave your mouth.

Thinking Cap

If this ever happens to you, try on a new thinking cap, one that's a little more sophisticated than the one you wore in first grade but holds the same good intentions. Your grownup thinking cap won't necessarily be a license to daydream, but it will help you shift from a hurried moment to one that needs some thought and reflection.

Putting on your thinking cap can help you block out the static that can get in the way and postpone—or even eliminate—your chance to examine and reflect. Sometimes you may forget to think. The static becomes white noise, like a faint headache, that you begin to tolerate and simply live with. It's like tuning into the same radio station despite the bad reception.

In our fast-paced lives, we forget that it's OK to pause and consider what we want to say. In a job interview, for instance, we may be so intent upon immediately answering a question that we forget to think about our response first. We're so focused on filling the few seconds of silence that we rush toward an end that actually diminishes our chances of making the favorable impression that is so important to us.

It's the same with our conversations. We finish someone's sentence. Or just when someone needs our full attention, we interrupt with our own experiences, pushing the other person's point of view into a far-off corner. And when we do stop to listen, we're thinking only of what to say next. As a college student, I used to talk way too much at parties. It's as if I equated my silence with looking stupid, as if not saying much meant I didn't have a lot to say.

As I grew up, I realized that thinking and listening hold tremendous value. As a writer, those tools are the lifeline of my work.

I once heard someone say that if you listen to a person you've just met, letting her or him do most of the talking, when the "conversation" is over, you may be left thinking, "Hmm. That person had a lot to say." The individual, however, may tell the next person she or he sees, "I just talked to the most interesting person," all because you decided to listen.

Sometimes stopping to think feels contrived and odd, as if the audio doesn't match the action. It's sort of like remembering to take deep, deep breaths in times of stress. When I do remember to breathe, or when someone gently reminds me, it feels like a chore and a pleasure all at the same time. Though I have to cease what I'm doing, the slow intake of oxygen washes away the unease, making more room to relax and move forward again. Thinking is the same way. At first, you might be a little afraid or disturbed that you have to schedule time to think, that thinking doesn't come naturally. But like those deep breaths, thinking can help you find meaning in places you might not otherwise go.

Take One Minute to Think

Try this for one day: whenever something requires you to make a decision, take one full minute to think over your response. Whether it's something you ask yourself or a question posed by a friend or a colleague—including your boss—take sixty seconds to simply ruminate. Not only might you feel more confident with your answer, you're also likely to experience some peace, moments that you feel good about. If this works for you, try to incorporate this exercise into your everyday routine until it becomes second nature. These few moments sprinkled throughout your days could lead you toward living a more fulfilled life. Who knows? Maybe this is what our teachers had in mind in the first place.

50 Don't Forget

"Memory is the diary we all carry about with us."

—MARY H. WALDRIP, IN *READER'S DIGEST* (1979)

I PROBABLY SAY "DON'T FORGET" a thousand times a day—"Don't forget to brush your teeth." "Don't forget your homework." "Don't forget to turn off the TV." Yet sometimes I can't even remember why I've walked into the kitchen. But some things I will never forget.

For instance, I'll never forget my neighbor Albert Stein—aka "Albird"—who used to bobby pin curly wood shavings to my impossibly straight hair. Or his wife, Jay, who washed my hair in her kitchen sink while I chewed on green licorice. I'll always remember the feeling of surprise and exhilaration when my sister, Wendy, taught me to ride a two-wheeler. I still recall the day when hours of practice culminated in that one proud and terrifying moment when she released her grip. I just kept going down the street, all the way to the corner.

When we take time to remember, we allow ourselves to slow down and reconnect with the moments and people who brought us to where we are today. It's not unlike the walk that follows an intense run. This emotional cooling down period enables us to put our feet back on the ground. Sometimes, we become so entwined in a situation that we forget how we got there in the first place. Those are the times when we literally ask ourselves, "How did I get to this point?" Once you've climbed the corporate ladder, you may forget what it's like to be young and working for the first time. Recalling this perspective can be handy if you're trying to motivate new college graduates. If you have children and can't understand why they won't do what you ask, remembering your own rebelliousness could give you a swift perspective and enhance your parenting skills. Remembering—going back in time—helps us to reorder what's important.

Our memories represent a composite of ourselves. Our experiences—joys and pains—define who and why we are. Recalling a happy memory can rekindle feelings of joy. We forget sometimes the power that such memories wield. Remembering a past kindness, for instance, can take the sting out of a present-day heartache. The memory may also be instructive, reminding us of how easy it is to be kind.

Remembering our pain can also teach us something important about ourselves. When we remember and then work through our hurts, we allow them to heal. Covering old wounds is just another way of denying who we are and what we want to become. Just as someone earns her wrinkles because she has lived, we earn who we are by all that we've experienced—our joys, our pains, our sorrows. It is only when we come to terms with painful memories that we can begin the process of extracting them from our pasts.

One of the best ways to remember is to remember with someone else. When we share our collective memories, we honor our relationships with the friends and family who have been part of our life journeys. One weekend, a few years ago, I soaked up the company of my old camp friends in Maryland's intoxicating Catoctin

Mountains. We'd come for a reunion, so we were prepared to reminisce.

Settling down to talk on the cabin porch, we naturally fell into our old vocabulary. The physical distance that dogs us year after year seemed to evaporate right into the huge and towering trees. The smells flooded my memory. Wood buildings that have stood for close to a century still filled the air with the same natural scent to which I'd been introduced so many years before.

For me, the weekend's finest moment occurred at a spot that quite unexpectedly engendered the loudest laughs and the warmest glow. With paper cups and champagne, a few of us gathered at the Round House, a sort of painter's haven on stilts. When we were kids, anything on a canvas became a masterpiece there. On this night, though, the canvas was our collective memories—memories that each of us had tended to and watched over during the course of our lives away from Camp Louise. It was as if we'd all set free the same butterfly and it loved us enough to return to us all. As we delved into the past, I felt as if in that perfect moment, we were all in the right place at the right time.

Reconnecting with your past provides a quiet understanding of how you got to where you are today. It can also give you another layer of comfort, not unlike a light blanket thrown on a bed for a little extra warmth. You can hook up with the past in several ways. Take out some photographs, and instead of worrying about the fact that you haven't put them in an album, just pore over the images and let your emotions rock back and forth. Dig out an old family recipe and do some cooking. You might even unearth the original handwritten instructions. Chances are this comfort food will make you feel good. As you're slipping and sliding down all your memory lanes, remember, too, to silently thank those who were kind. This French proverb probably says it best: gratitude is the heart's memory.

51 Call in Sick

"The happiest people in this world are the convalescents."

—MARY ADAMS, *CONFESSIONS OF A WIFE* (1902)

SOME DAYS ARE BETTER SPENT UNDER THE COVERS with a mug of chicken soup. Your throat is raw, your head is pounding, and you can't remember your middle name. Plus, there happens to be a really good movie on at 11:00 A.M. This is a day to call in sick.

Sometimes, though, you don't even have to be sick to take a sick day. You might be feeling blue. Or perhaps a giant deadline is just too much to face; regrouping at home with a hot cup of tea could be just what you need to tackle your work—one day later. Once you finally decide to call in sick, after you've wrestled with the guilt, you'll feel terrific. Well, maybe not terrific; after all, you've just called in sick. You will feel better though, and you'll probably get the rest you need to face reality the next day.

When we were kids, it was much easier to call in sick. Guilt was usually the last thing on our minds. Besides, we didn't have to call school; our parents usually took care of that. I recall the moments of truth when my mother, after reading the thermometer, would deliver two of the happiest words I could ever hope to hear: *no school*. Even in the midst of a feverish slump, I could feel my body enjoy a fleeting moment of extraordinary delight—relief, too.

In those days, we didn't hear those haunting words whispering in our heads: "You've got too much to do" or "You wimp! Get out there and work!" No, this was easy. These days, though, we have to work very hard at calling in sick. Perhaps you slip some self-pity into your voice to assure a boss that you really do feel crummy. You also can add words like *contagious* and *bacteria* to maximize your credibility.

These days, most of us don't get fevers very often. We've grown immune to a lot of the things that used to knock us cold. And, if you're unlucky like me, you rarely hear others suggesting that you call in sick. Still, you may have those days when you just want to wave a white flag and surrender to whatever's invaded your system. Unfortunately, surrendering to just one day of healing isn't so easy to do. It's hard to step away from daily demands.

Nevertheless, vestiges of those sick days I loved years ago are still with me. For example, I relish the thought of hunkering down under a down quilt with a cup of hot tea, a movie or book, and the prospect of falling into a deep, midday sleep. Puttering around the house is an acceptable sick-day activity as well.

Regardless of its regenerative and therapeutic characteristics, the periodic sick day is still elusive and simply difficult to build into our day-to-day routine. No one really likes to get sick, and admitting to ourselves that we need to rest to get better is akin to scheduling a root canal just in case.

As exhilarating and dynamic as it is to lead a nonstop life—even when it helps ward off a cold or trick a scratchy throat into an early departure—trying to run at the same frenzied rate when our bodies crave a breather simply isn't worth the race. Sometimes it's not easy to distinguish between a need to heal from a physical malady and a need to simply take yourself off the hook for a day.

Think back to your own childhood, when the person looking after you could, in a split second, decide what was best: forging ahead and muddling through or taking six hours off to allow your breathing to be steady, your throat to be soothed, and your eyes to close at the drop of a soupspoon.

Just because you call it quits for one day doesn't mean you don't know how (or want) to live life to its fullest. And just because you decide to stay in bed for one day with your favorite coughing elixir close by doesn't mean that you're inadequate or can't hack it. Calling in sick— even if it's to yourself versus your boss downtown—is about accepting limits and knowing when to stop. Not forever. And probably not even for an entire week. But for one day, imagine that the best medicine of all is a good dose of rest and relaxation. It could be the magic cure after all.

Get Well Soon

So she was a little late, but generally speaking Little Red Riding Hood had her heart in the right place when she skipped off into the woods to deliver a basket of goodies to her ailing grandmother. You can do the same for a friend *and* avoid a nasty encounter with a wolf. If someone you know is suffering with a cold or flu (or anything that's knocked them flat), assemble some goodies that are especially good for the weak and faint of heart. Take a pretty ceramic mug, and fill it with honey cough drops, herbal teas, cotton handkerchiefs, and a few capsules of time-released vitamin C. Add a pint of chicken soup from your favorite delicatessen (or your own recipe) and a box of tissues for a truly heartwarming special delivery.

52 Ice Cream for Breakfast

"All happiness is a form of innocence."

—MARGUERITE YOURCENAR, *ALEXIS* (1929)

ICE CREAM FOR BREAKFAST is about assuming a childlike optimism and getting away with fun. It's about knowing a thing or two when it comes to breaking the rules. It's about treating yourself to what really matters.

When you eat a little ice cream for breakfast—or pancakes for supper or licorice for lunch—you sample a thin slice of heaven. If you do it enough, it could change your outlook. When you add ice cream to your life's diet—especially when it's consumed in the morning—you find out quickly what's really important. It's as if you're living each day at a time, as if the next day is your last day, but without the gloom and doom. It is appreciating life's small pleasures.

Years ago, for Sandy, a woman I met the other day, ice cream for breakfast meant something different appeared on her kitchen table. When she ran out of milk, she turned to that other carton of calcium and topped her kids' morning cereal with generous scoops of ice cream. For Jeannie, a freelance writer living in Switzerland, ice cream for breakfast means treating herself, almost nightly, to a local brand of chocolate-riddled granola.

For others, ice cream for breakfast is, more than anything, a state of mind. My friend Laura once exclaimed over dinner, "My life is ice cream for breakfast!" And although some ice cream could be compared to the crown jewels, eating it for breakfast goes way beyond acquiring the finer things in life. Rather, ice cream for breakfast is more about achieving what you can't always hold within your hands. It's having the guts to say "I hated that movie!" when everyone else is giving it a thumbs up. It's realizing that there is wisdom in and truth to the notion that you really have to take care of yourself if you're going to take care of others.

Eating ice cream for breakfast isn't about sticking with one diet. Consuming the same thing day in and day out gets dull. Choices become meaningless. Pleasures become elusive and sometimes disappear altogether. At the core of *Ice Cream for Breakfast* is your ability to buck convention and to question what's good for you and what makes you happy. Those who eat ice cream for breakfast don't live against the same setting every day. They rely, instead, upon a variety of backdrops. Like an elaborate theatrical production, the scenes change and the characters move on and off the stage.

Ice cream for breakfast also implies a certain lawlessness. It's the feeling you got when you found something that wasn't yours. You'd slyly look around, scoop it up, and skip away singing, "Finders keepers! Losers weepers!" It's remembering how it felt to live through a moment completely disconnected with your normal routine or what you'd come to expect: your mother surprising you with a toy you'd thought you'd never get; the teacher announcing that recess would last all afternoon; the team captain picking you first instead of last.

Ice cream for breakfast is admitting that small pleasures are often enough. It's about remembering the sound of the ice cream truck rumbling down your street and buying, for well under a dollar, what your mother never brought home from the grocery store. It's buying a madras handbag simply because it reminds you of the one you carried in the sixth grade. It's remembering how good it felt to climb up into a tree and settle in with a good book. Ice cream for breakfast is about deciding for yourself what's important and what's not. It's about listening to the most important voice of all—your own.

Author's Note

Do you eat ice cream for breakfast? Do you ever break the rules in order to have more fun? Tell me in an E-mail: icecream4break@aol.com. I'd be honored to hear your stories. Also, you can visit me at www.leslielevine.com. Thanks, too, for reading *Ice Cream for Breakfast*.